THE REALITY OF REJECTION

The
REALITY
of
REJECTION

It is real.
It is painful.
It is ugly . . .

but it NEVER has to define your life again!

MELISSA CADE GARCIA

Transformative
CONNECTIONS

Published by Transformative Connections, LLC
Fort Myers, Florida

Cover and Interior Design by Imagine!® Studios
www.ArtsImagine.com

Cover Images: iStock.com/Nikki Zalewski, stock.adobe.com/baddesigner
Interior Images: stock.adobe.com/leremy, stock.adobe.com/Trifonenko Ivan, stock.adobe.com/Amy Louise Baker/Wirestock Creators, stock.adobe.com/SriWidiawati

Note to Readers: This publication contains the opinions and ideas of its author. It is intended to provide helpful and informative material on the subjects addressed in the publication. It is sold with the understanding that the author and publisher are not engaged in rendering medical, health, or any kind of personal, or professional services in the book. The reader should consult with his or her medical, health, or other professional before adopting any suggestions in this book or drawing inferences from it.

Names and identifying details of some of the people portrayed in this book have been changed.

ISBN: 979-8-9895512-0-0 (paperback)
ISBN: 979-8-9895512-1-7 (e-book)

Library of Congress Control Number: 2023951348

First printing: December 2023

TABLE OF CONTENTS

Section 1
THE TRUTH ABOUT REJECTION
1

CHAPTER ONE

CHAPTER TWO

CHAPTER THREE

CHAPTER FOUR

Section 2
THE TOXICITY OF REJECTION
57

CHAPTER FIVE

CHAPTER SIX

Section 3
THE TRIUMPH OVER REJECTION
107

To my beautiful mother, who gave me life and courage;
to my amazing husband, who gave me love and encouragement;
and to my beloved Jesus, who gave me peace and a purpose.

AUTHOR'S NOTE

An incredibly wise person said, "God gives us one face, and we give ourselves another." William Shakespeare's quote prompted a question. Why would we choose to be different than what our Creator intended? I have discovered that most of us do not even realize that we are far from who God has called us to be. If you look closely, you can see it in others quite easily. How about in our own self-reflection? Can we be bold enough to look within and be honest about what we may discover? Most responses would range from "I am as real as it gets" to "Maybe I'm a little off track, but I am a pretty authentic person." The unconscious reality is that many of us change our behavior to fit in. You see, we were created for connection. The desire for it is so strong many bend their reactions, responses, and, at times, their character to appease the judgment of others, eager to connect. Our souls are altered with every twist and turn. And when our efforts to connect are rejected, it leads to a loss of hope, leaving us hesitant to try again in the future. Ironically, the rejection of our pasts rules our actions in the present due to the fear of reliving the rejection that got us to put on the invisible mask to begin with.

PREFACE

Collaborating and working with people over the years, professionally and ministerially, has allowed me to witness, address, and study the problems and solutions to the rejection epidemic through two different lenses: secularly and spiritually. Although I am sure there will be some in these arenas that may object, you will find both perspectives intentionally addressed throughout the following chapters.

First, I understand that rejection hits everyone at some time or another, no matter who you are. God has placed enormous potential in every single human being on this planet, and I believe everyone should have the opportunity to discover that potential for themselves. Secondly, I share both sides because each holds its own nuggets of gold, and no matter what your perspective may be, both can bless you on your journey to healing. Finally, my faith is the foundation of my life. My relationship with Jesus and the profound discoveries in His word has brought me to this point of restoration. However, this did not happen overnight for me. Not only did the process take time, but it took over a decade before I decided to surrender my heart and life to Him. God is a gentleman and does not force anyone to follow Him. The gift of free will is beautiful, and everyone deserves the right to choose for themselves. I am simply a messenger of the truths I have lived and learned, but I share them joyfully with anyone seeking to discover this freedom for themselves.

INTRODUCTION

Other than grieving the loss of a loved one, there is perhaps no worse feeling in life than that of being rejected. The feeling that we are unwanted or unwelcomed hurts regardless of whether it comes from family, friends, a coworker, or just an acquaintance. And it doesn't matter if it is relayed through words, actions, or the absence of either one. On a superficial level, with those we barely know, the rejection stings. If the rejecter is someone we love, trust, or both, the pain hits at a deeper level and will usually leave a long-lasting scar.

All of us, at some point in our lives, have experienced this pain. We probably even know people in our family or social circles who seemingly have never recovered from it. Perhaps you are that person. Maybe it transpired over time or unexpectedly hit you like a ton of bricks. You still do not clearly understand precisely what happened or why, but there is no doubt that something inside your soul simply seems fragmented. No matter how hard you try, you cannot seem to shake yourself from the subconscious idea that you somehow are not enough. Perhaps even graver is the constant replay of the memories and wounds of your past.

At times, you may find yourself feeling incapacitated, unable to function the way you would like. You cannot put your finger on it, but you have a sense that you are somehow different from others. You may even describe what you experience as a numbness to your emotions. If you are on the other end of the emotional spectrum, you could find yourself consumed with feelings of anger and bitterness. The biggest indicator is that peace seems to escape you. Worst of all, you feel utterly stuck in this uncontrollable and overwhelming rut. It is as if you are living in a mental prison, and the keys you need to escape are nowhere to be found. I have good news for you. With courage, patience, and persistence, you can be set free. Free to be the person God has called you to be.

Helping people grow and develop themselves and the relationships they have been blessed with is at the heart of why I chose the professional and ministerial path I continue to travel on today. Through more than thirty years in education, counseling, and coaching, I have been honored to serve individuals of all ages from all walks of life. My greatest pleasure has come from witnessing them grow leaps and bounds as they find the strength to break free from fixed mindsets and discover who they truly are and what they are capable of doing.

However, the most immense sorrow has been in meeting those with great potential but poisoned and paralyzed so profoundly by life's past rejections they were not able to realize the freedom intended for us all. Like most of us, they too sensed the lack of peace but had no clue what was happening inside their soul. Their only escape was to attempt to numb the chaos.

Many have turned to alcohol, drugs, pornography, and countless other forms of destruction in hopes of easing their pain. Some were not so obvious; they hid their deep-seated agony in other ways. Some desperately sought attention, even when it was at the expense of their good name. Others, constantly surrounded by drama and tension, no matter where they went, never willing to admit that they were the constant in every conflict that plagued them. These individuals were oblivious to the pain they were causing themselves and the people they loved.

While it is true that I have long studied the subject of rejection, the long-lasting effects, and the healing promises, my true expertise comes from the fact that I have lived through the pain, consequences, and victories myself. Like many of you, much of it came as an innocent spectator, naïvely standing in the line of fire and wounded by the choices of the very people God brought into my life to love and protect me. They had also gotten caught in the jaws of rejection.

In my latter years, I discovered the most significant lessons on the subject from many of their lives. One of them, my greatest hero, was my mother. She was physically abandoned by her birth father, emotionally neglected in her marriage, and psychologically desolated by the disease of dementia. Another was my husband, who grew up without his father or mother but was graciously raised by his elderly grandparents as their own. Additionally, my father grew up in a verbally and physically abusive home, where love was overshadowed by the weight of rejection. At the young age of fourteen, with very few resources, he decided it was safer to do life on his own.

While there is no question today that God's favor was on me when he connected me with these beautiful souls, the hurt and pain of the rejection they carried beneath the surface reared its head throughout their lives. Sadly, it was poured out in various detrimental ways, affecting those around them, including me.

After much prayer and reflection, I encountered a Divine awareness of life's parallels to the troubles and triumphs surrounding us. These discoveries have brought me insight and healing from my past and a necessary understanding for the future. I hope the written illustrations shared will touch your soul in the same way.

In this book, we will examine many truths surrounding rejection. As these realities are uncovered, you will begin to see yourself outside of the picture frame. This perspective of standing on the outside looking in will provide you with a better understanding of why it happens and how it can affect each person's life differently. More importantly, my desire is that the words you find on the pages of this book may bring clarity and discernment for you and the people you love, who may also be suffering silently from their buried wounds.

If the pain of rejection has touched you personally, my prayer is that you will be able to identify the toxic signs that have tainted your life but, up until now, have gone undetected. Above all else, may you find the courage to choose to break free from the destructive control of this unfair yet unavoidable offense and discover the resolve to never allow the pain of rejection to control your life or define who you are ever again. It is in this freedom that you will find the power to love freely and finally discover the truth about who God intended you to be. You, too, deserve to be set free and live a life of peace.

Section 1

THE TRUTH
ABOUT
REJECTION

CHAPTER ONE

REJECTION IS RARELY ABOUT YOU

"Two percent of people think; three percent of people think they think; and ninety-five percent of people would rather die than think."

GEORGE BERNARD SHAW

Standing under the steady stream of scalding water, I sobbed uncontrollably, hoping somehow the shower would wash away the mess I had gotten myself into. The overwhelming confusion I felt at that moment paled in comparison to the disbelief and disappointment that consumed me. Disbelief in the situation I was in and disappointed in myself for allowing it to happen. Just when I thought there was a glimpse of light at the end of the tunnel, I managed to fall back into the pit of darkness. With the water temperature as hot as my body could bear, I prayed the tests were wrong.

At the very young age of twenty-one and on the tail end of an ugly divorce, I found myself with a positive pregnancy test. This was the second one I had taken at the neighborhood clinic because somehow, I knew the first one just had to be wrong. The mortification I felt led to hopelessness. This just could not be. After escaping a very toxic marriage, there was no way I was prepared to jump into another serious relationship, and I certainly was not ready to be a mother. All I could do was beg God to make it go away.

LOOKING OUT FOR #1

If I am being honest, selfishness bred the fear and doubt that was driving my thinking that day. What would people say about me? I was barely out of one bad marriage, and now I was pregnant. How was I going to raise a child by myself? After all the court costs and having to take on joint financial responsibilities alone, I was pretty close to broke. How was this going to affect my future plans? I wanted to return to school, but working two jobs made it very difficult. An unplanned baby was not going to make it any easier. All the thoughts that ran through my head were centered around me, my inconveniences, and my unwanted outcomes. In that moment, not once did I consider the precious, innocent life I was carrying inside.

The definition of selfishness reads like this: the quality of thinking of only your advantage.

You may be second-guessing yourself right now asking if you picked up the right book. You did. You see, in order to examine the realities of rejection, we must establish that selfishness can often be at the center of the rejection we all at one time have had to endure. The rejector usually has one person on their mind, and it is themselves. If you have been stung by the pain of rejection, rest assured you were the last thing on the offender's mind.

The truth is humanity is primarily made up of people of impulse, people whose eyes are set on themselves alone. These so-called rejectors are driven by emotion and self-centered satisfaction. They do what feels good in the moment and what serves them best. This can be true whether you are a person of faith and adhere to the Bible, which tells us that everyone is born with a sinful nature, or you are more philosophical in nature and believe that ego drives our selfish decisions.

Not too long ago, while in the middle of an observation, I sat in a classroom full of eleven- and twelve-year-old students who mostly confirmed that this is how most of us are wired. Their teacher posed a question that required critical thinking and some self-reflection. It went like this: *You have two slices of pizza in front of you, and two of your friends come over. You are asked to share the pizza, but you cannot cut the slices. What would you do?*

Having worked in education for over thirty years, I can tell you children are very honest. Over half of the students said they would eat both slices because they were asked, not told, to share the pizza. A couple said to avoid conflict, no one would get any pizza. Out of a class of eighteen students, there were only two selfless responses. One said he would ask one of the friends to cut his slice in half and share it since there was no rule about the friends splitting it. Pretty clever problem solving, in my opinion. The other said he would give each friend a slice and find something else to eat for himself. Close to ninety percent focused on number one: themselves.

This seems to be a pattern that continues into adulthood. It is every man for himself. As a matter of fact, we live in a society where some people are told that they have to step on others to get to the top. A dog-eat-dog world. All of this feeds into the selfish part of our humanity. In fact, a whole line of thinking says this is the way to be if you want to succeed in life. While I have to admit that I lived on this premise myself for many years, it is my belief now that this is, in fact, the most miserable way to live. It is not that looking out for ourselves is a complete loss. There is indeed some credibility to that philosophy. Realistically speaking, it isn't easy to care for others when we have yet to learn to take care of ourselves. The problem is that when your focus is totally set on you alone, it tends to create an inconsiderate, defensive individual who finds fault everywhere they go.

IT'S NOT ABOUT YOU

One fact that people find hard to understand or believe deserves to be highlighted. When rejection strikes, it is rare that the rejecter did it with the intent of malice towards you. Yes, you read that correctly. The rejection seldom has anything to do with you. I know it sounds strange since the offended human soul naturally tends to become discouraged or angry and respond accordingly in defense of the hurt they have just experienced. In the natural mind, when we feel the pain of rejection, we want to retaliate, defend ourselves, and give them a dose of what they gave us.

On a practical but hypothetical level, the reality is that the waitress probably had her own personal issues she was dealing with when she gave you an unpleasant attitude. You may have triggered her behavior, but it really had nothing to do with you and everything to do with the rebellious teenage son who refuses to respect her or lift a finger to help her out at home. If her own son is being disrespectful, it is quite likely she is reeling from a personal rejection of her very own. Maybe it was the tone you used to complain about your meal. It reminded her of the rejection from her very own child and caused her to snap at you.

Believe it or not, this is true at even more personal levels with the ones we love and hold close to our hearts. Their actions or inactions are likely a result of their internal battles that are not visible to the naked eye. The person you see as bad, their horrible actions or overreactions, are in direct response to how they see their world and are responding through their scars. Like you and I, the "rejecter's view" is shaped by their past experiences, which gives life to their current expectations.

PERSPECTIVE PAINTS THE PICTURE

When I was in elementary school, one of my classmate's braveries fascinated me. Aside from being one of the kindest people I had ever met, Amanda loved to show off her little crooked index finger. The deformity of the skinny appendage came from a snake bite. As she recalled the story to the group of attentive ten-year-olds, me included, she dared to chase the slithering creature behind a thick bush in her backyard. When she finally got her hands on it and picked it up, the snake was pretty agitated, so naturally, it bit her. I am guessing the snake was not poisonous, or Amanda would not have made it to fifth grade to share her tale (pun intended).

Her parents were wilderness buffs, so being drawn to the outdoors and all its different varieties of life was second nature to her. During recess, she would casually pick up giant creepy insects with her bare hands and hold them out on display for everyone to see. It was the moment she scooped up a horrendous hairy wolf spider and tried to stroke its back that I knew in my mind that Amanda was not a normal human being.

You see, in my home, spiders were monsters. My mother was the only soul in our family brave enough to deal with them. This included my father, who passed the fear gene to me and my siblings. Everyone else in my childhood home was terrified of the creepy creatures, no matter how big or small. You can bet money that no one in our house would ever knowingly get close to a spider, much less consider picking it up. The way we saw it, if Dad, brave and strong in our mind, ran in the opposite direction of an arachnid, then there was no reason for his children not to do the same thing. Amanda's perspective on spiders was different than mine. Not because one of us was better than the other but because our experiences and memories of our view of spiders were shaped before we even realized it.

PERSPECTIVE PICKS THE PREFERENCE

When rejection rears its head, understand that it could be as simple as the rejecter holding a different set of beliefs or values. Take a dating situation, for instance. Maybe the first gal to ever catch his eye and steal his heart was a brunette with beautiful brown eyes. The fact that he does not give you a second glance when most males are instantly drawn to your baby blues and golden blonde hair most likely has to do with the experience of his youth.

This is how most of our ideas of people, places and things are formed. At least initially. We tend to love or hate things according to our first experiences. If we have a terrible incident with a dog, then we are prone to be afraid of them. On the other hand, if we have a pleasant experience with a canine, we may very well become dog lovers.

Typically, the rule is if there is a high emotion attached to a memory or an event, it becomes part of who we are or what we believe. It is a life perspective, per se, and it dictates a person's attitude, ideas, and how they approach certain aspects of the world around them. In the dating world, many lose so much sleep over the fact that someone they may have found attractive shows little to no interest in them. A person will toss and turn, questioning what they did wrong or wondering what is wrong with them when it has nothing to do with them. Ironically, this type of self-doubt comes from a programmed perspective garnered somewhere in the "rejected" individual's own past.

This is not to say that either perspective is set in stone. People change the way they see things all the time. However, the person must be open to change. It must come through an intentional effort on their part. The "change" usually comes when the person feels they are be-tween a rock and a hard place, with few alternatives. At the very least, the effects of a soul-stirring confrontation, such as the possibility of losing someone, could prompt a person to consider an adjustment in their original viewpoint.

PERSISTENCE DOES NOT ALWAYS PAY

The reality, however, is that this does not often happen. Most people are so attached to their perspective they will go out of their way to prove opposers wrong. Many times, this is where a person facing what they see as a rejection will dig themselves deeper into a hole instead of simply walking away. These are individuals who are determined to get a yes at all costs. Some may consider this type of persistence an excellent strategy for going after what you want.

While this may be reasonable in the professional world occasionally, it is a breeding ground for starting a toxic relationship bond. If someone turns them down, they take it personally and see the rejection as a sign of their value and worth. When this is the case, quite often, it stems from insecurity.

I have witnessed men and women who have run themselves ragged, trying to convince another person that they are worthy of acceptance when it was never about them to begin with. It was about the other person's point of view, likely forged by those who had the most influence over them when they were younger.

The most heartbroken clients I have counseled were searching for a reprieve from damage brought on by these types of relationships. A particular young lady recalled the beginning stages of one such partnership. Against the advice of almost everyone who cared about her, she happily entered into a five-year destructive dance with someone who saw a world totally different from hers. She had a background of strong family ties, and her parents' provided encouragement and support at every turn. They taught her that if God had placed a desire in her heart to achieve, He also would equip her with all she needed to reach her goals. To say she saw a world filled with endless possibilities was an understatement. Like most of these sad stories, her relationship began with a whirlwind of romance that was short-lived.

Extreme measures of flattery and devotion are how a narcissist will entangle their prey (we will delve more into narcissism later). While true, most people tend to introduce themselves with the intention of impressing those whose attention they wish to catch. Think about how many bad hires have happened through the guise of first impressions. Narcissist or not, the problem comes when the other person turns a blind eye to the facts once reality comes to light.

In the first few weeks, the young lady in question believed she had found the man of her dreams. He doted on her hand and foot. Yet, sometime in the second month, the man she was dating subtly began to drop the act. Admittedly, she said it was probably sooner. She was always someone who saw the glass as half-full and people as ultimately good in nature. This partially led to her failing to accept the truth that stood before her eyes. He, on the other hand, believed the glass he was given was broken and everyone was out to get him. Their outlook on life was on opposite ends of the spectrum. He would ridicule her enthusiasm for life and insult her creative ideas. Instead of his constant rejection of who she was deterring her, she resolved to stand firm.

After he succeeded at alienating her from her most vital support system, everything else went downhill. She regrettably admitted she should have run away at the sign of the first red flag. Instead, she even entertained an idea he planted in her head, "Perhaps your father is not as great as you think he is."

The first part of her defense was that she was taught to believe the best in people. The irony was that despite the unsavory doubt he was feeding her, she continued to believe this man was good, even though he prompted her to question the very man who had raised her. The second part of her defense was that because this man had good in him, she could convince him to see the world from her point of view. She banked on the fact that their start together was magical, as brief as it was. She believed she could get him back to the place where he had her on a pedestal. Back before he rejected her, another narcissistic trick.

To make a long story short, she spent over five years in a relationship that got worse by the day and nearly destroyed her. She was constantly put down and demeaned; she lost the joy of life, put her goals on the back burner, and, worst of all, she did not even recognize herself at the end of the torturous rollercoaster ride. The idea that she could change how another person saw the world did not fare well for her. The repeated rejections led her to question everything she believed. Ultimately, this man's words and actions reflected a horrible perspective of his own self-centered world.

Although in the beginning his treatment of the young lady said nothing about her, the fact that she chose to stay because she believed she could change him led to the tragic consequences she endured. Acknowledging the red flag of rejection for what it was at the start of the relationship would have saved her a great deal of heartache.

SELF-CENTEREDNESS CAN SOLIDIFY PERSPECTIVE

If you are familiar with the world of memes, you have probably come across the picture of a number drawn on the floor where two individuals are standing on opposite sides, facing each other. One sees the number 9, while the other sees the number 6. Both people stand firm, insisting that their viewpoint is correct. If either individual went around to the other person's side, they would see why they believe the way they do. As individuals begin to mature in their natural development, there tends to be a better appreciation of the differences in the world around them. They may not necessarily ever agree with the other side, but the attempt to look outside themselves creates a sense

of understanding for the opposing view. Thus avoiding a perceived display of rejection.

However, many people never outgrow their tunnel vision, seeming only aware of what is before them. All their energy and talent, if not most of it, is spent on what they deem important, and ninety-nine out of a hundred times, they are at the top of their priority list. They tend to focus on a single point of view—their own.

In its juvenile stages, this is the start of what is known as self-awareness. Self-awareness is considered one of the buzzwords in the current mindset culture that we are in. Yet, it is much more than just a simple catchphrase. It is a powerful skill to develop and essential to who you are as a person. While the opinion is still out on whether we are born self-aware, the fact that it is a part of us that grows and develops during the first few years of life is unquestionable.

A baby, for instance, will often be amused if you place a mirror in front of them. After a while, they will come to the understanding that the face they see in the mirror's reflection is actually their own. This infant will live the first years of his life simply focusing on himself. What he wants and what he needs are the center of his world. It has nothing to do with selfishness but everything to do with the limits of what he knows. It is merely human instinct; this internal self-awareness is a normal part of a child's makeup.

Research shows that there are distinct levels of self-awareness. Suppose this same child continues to develop without any critical or stressful interruptions in his life. In that case, his self-awareness will mature him into an adult who can monitor his own thoughts and feelings with a robust capacity to build healthy relationships. Ideally, each healthy developmental stage will lead to the next.

The sad news, however, is that few people live a trouble-free childhood. Some of you reading this will be able to attest to this truth. These innocent children enter into the sphere of unstable people, and they end up consumed by parental divorces, abandonment, addictions, and deaths. Others may encounter physical, verbal, emotional, or sexual abuse. These tragedies mark them with a collection of confused feelings, leaving the child traumatized and quite often emotionally shattered or calloused. Something inside the child searches for ways to protect himself against future trauma. Unfortunately, many get caught in this stage. Therefore, they never quite outgrow the self-centered perspective of their infancy.

Whether it is a hardened attitude offended by everything or from the fragile view of their victimhood, these individuals, consciously or subconsciously, stay focused and tuned into keeping themselves safe from further pain. Sadly, as adults, these people will leak the residue of rejection everywhere they go.

HIGH E.Q. LEADS TO LOW REJECTION

In a perfect world, what should happen next as the child matures past the internal self-awareness stage is the unfolding of an external self-awareness. There is a lot to be said about these two perspectives of humanity. Both, in a healthy state, can open the door to a robust and balanced life. They also are a component of what is recognized in the world of psychology as a person's E.Q., also known as emotional intelligence or emotional quotient. E.Q., which gauges an individual's emotional health, should not be confused with I.Q., a measure of someone's intelligence.

To be clear, having a high I.Q. while having a low E.Q. is possible. Although quite academically intelligent, these individuals can fall on two ends of the spectrum. They can unwittingly dish out actions and words that seem to rebuke or reject people at every turn, or on the other hand, they can have difficulty reading other people's intentions.

When I was in high school, Susie, one of my classmates, was extremely book-smart. If you gave her a test, you could bet your bank account she was going to ace it. Her high I.Q. got her a full ride to Florida State University. However, this gal's E.Q. was a different story. I did not know her well enough to form an opinion on what experiences produced this gap between her I.Q. and E.Q., but it sure did cause plenty of problems in her social life. By no means was she a terrible person. Susie did not have the necessary internal resources to spot repeated red flags in her choice of relationships. This, unfortunately, positioned her for recurring rejection, and she was often taken advantage of.

A person's emotional intelligence (E.Q.) can be summed up as the ability to monitor and identify one's emotions and those of others, while correctly using the information as a guide on how to proceed in their thinking and responses. It should also be noted that people with a combination of a high I.Q. and E.Q. tend to be more personally and professionally successful.

Moreover, if you face rejection from someone with a high E.Q., they have quite likely given much consideration to your feelings in the matter. Even so, their decision is without question, based on their perspective, and has nothing to do with your value as a person.

If rejection seems to come easily from specific individuals, meaning they nonchalantly ignore, insult, offend, or abuse you, consider it their problem and understand that you desperately need to steer clear of them. I will remind you that there is a great likelihood that their emotional growth was stunted at the beginning levels of self-awareness, and they cannot see past their self-centered outlook. This person most certainly would score low on the E.Q. scale. Even so, spending time trying to change their perspective when they are unwilling to see past themselves should be considered time wasted. Either way, their rejection says more about them than it does about the person being rejected.

RESTORATION

After all the emotional turmoil I experienced in my early twenties while facing an unplanned pregnancy during a very dark time, I can report a happy ending to this story. I understand that this may be a sensitive topic for some, but know this: God's grace extends beyond our human frailties and the choices we make. The truth is life leads us all down unexpected paths, and we all carry our individual burdens that others cannot see or begin to comprehend.

Thinking back thirty years ago, as I wrestled with all the "what ifs" of the future, the emotions and confusion were overwhelming. My heart breaks for those who have found themselves in a similar situation, burdened by the grief of having to make life-altering decisions. Let me just say that what transpired next was only through the grace of God.

Together with the baby's father, who is now my wonderful husband, we made a decision to put ourselves aside and do our best to make life work for this innocent unborn child. It was a decision that would shape our future in ways we could never imagine. We gave birth to an absolutely beautiful little girl who, even to this day, can light up any room she walks into. A few years later, we welcomed another miracle, our son. Even though we have had our rough patches as a family, God has blessed us tremendously over the last three decades.

Yet, it cannot be denied that often, rejection's touch can leave a deep-rooted mark. The reality of this story is that my daughter, in all her innocence, faced rejection in the womb. While I have never regretted a day of her life, I have wondered if the emotional stress and emotions I experienced during that tumultuous time affected the innocent life I carried in any way.

Through some research, I found a 2010 study in a New Scientist article that had expectant mothers watch movie clips. During the clips that contained happy scenes, the unborn baby moved around a lot. On the contrary, when the mom watched a sad clip, the child was much more still, providing some proof that the mother's feelings affected the baby somehow.

Dr. Thomas Verny, author of The Secret Life of the Unborn Child, based his writing on six years of researching life in the womb. It is an incredible book based around scientific evidence "that the unborn child is a feeling, remembering, aware being," and what happens between conception and birth shapes a child's emotional development. He further notes that "the womb is the child's first world." If that world provides love and warmth, the child will be drawn to those things once they are born, and vice versa.

I rest in the fact that although the first few weeks of my daughter's conception were wrought with confusion and negativity, the greater part of her life was and continues to be filled with love and acceptance. As the first niece and granddaughter, she became the center of my family's world.

Looking back, I can say without a doubt that the person who existed at the age of twenty-one was a different individual. I lived in a place where my reaction to the unknown and discomfort was the typical fight or flight, but my main concern was looking out for number one.

Even in my inexperienced state of selfish preservation, I am grateful that God granted me the grace to look past myself.

Yet, if the science is valid, it is highly likely that my daughter felt a sense of rejection even before she was born. And just like most of us, the rejection had absolutely nothing to do with her. She was perfect in every sense of the word. Instead, it had everything to do with the self-centered perspective of the rejecter.

"He came to his own people, and even they rejected him."

JOHN 1:11

CHAPTER TWO

IT IS
UNAVOIDABLE

· *". . . offences will come . . ."*

LUKE 17:1 (KJV)

S tuck in a job I had outgrown, I waited as patiently as possible for my call back. My interview at the end of the previous week had gone pretty well. So well, it had left me feeling quite hopeful at the possibility of winning over the new position I had applied for. There were only two other candidates in the running, also a good sign. I had no reason to believe otherwise. Add that to the fact that I had a pretty good track record when it came to landing jobs after an interview.

Sure, I was young and had only held just a handful of positions. That did not negate the fact that up until this point, when it came to transitioning from one job to the next, all I had ever experienced were successes. Sounds boastful, I know, but this was my perspective at that moment. This perspective also added to my devastation when everything was said and done.

I was in my mid-20s looking for a way to positively impact the world, so I held the mindset that the place I had been employed for the past three years was a dead end for me. With no possibility for promotion and the loss of excitement in the work I was doing, my employment search record brought me much-needed optimism for the chance of finally being able to get out and start fresh somewhere else. Landing this dream job was my new mission in life. My heart was one hundred percent into this task.

This potential position was perfect because I would finally have the opportunity to work with the people in my community. What made it even better was that I would be involved in supporting local parents to increase their involvement in the schools their children attended. This meant that I would play a part in offering a chance for children to be more successful in their education. Knowing that I would be making a difference in the world around me made my future job even more significant.

My enthusiasm soared even more when my interviewer encouraged me to set up an appointment to get a license to transport passengers. You can believe there was no hesitation on my end since it would be part of my new responsibilities. This was yet another indicator that I was headed for a new place of employment. I picked up a study guide from the local DMV and studied it every chance I had. From where I stood, all the stars were aligned, so to say that my expectations were pretty high was an understatement. I was believing for the best. In my mind, the job was mine. There was no other way to look at it for me. As the saying goes, "It was so close, I could taste it."

REJECTION DEFINED

Rejection, whether talking about a person, an idea or a thing, is the simple act of dismissing or pushing away. It can happen so subtly that one may not even realize rejection has grazed them. On the other hand, the rebuff can be so obvious it seems to knock some people right off their feet; and, in some instances, change their very being. It is a part of life that, without a doubt, will touch every single human on the planet at some point. The levels of severity will tend to vary depending on the offense or the person being offended. If we look closely, this dismissal is all around us. Without giving it a second thought, every day people reject ideas, food, invitations, and, most regrettably, other people. Think about it; if something or someone is displeasing, the natural instinct is to push away.

In many instances, we are sometimes the rejecters. The root word reject in the dictionary makes this truth a bit clearer. You will find the definition explaining that the dismissal that arises from rejection is due to an inadequacy of failing to meet someone's standards or someone's tastes.

Think it through from your eyes. Why would you find yourself committing the act of rejection? It could be because something about a person does not sit quite well with you. You may have a preconceived idea about an individual that goes against your own liking. Your personality may clash with someone else's, or your preferences for life may be on opposite ends of the spectrum. Whatever the case, you simply do not feel a connection to the person in question. What follows, if the snubbed individual was expecting some type of positive response yet receives none, is a sense of ostracism. Whether we intended to or not, we have participated in the act of rejection.

You may ask yourself, "Am I expected to be drawn or to attempt to connect with every human being, no matter how appalled I may be by them?" The answer is, "Of course not." The point is that it happens to everyone and through everyone, whether we are conscious of it or not. Maybe you have a high awareness and are on the more considerate side. You make a careful effort not to sneer, or at the very least, you try your best to be cordial with individuals who may turn you off. The truth is, even though you were sympathetic to the person's feelings and tried your best not to be offensive, you have rejected them on the inside. While this is a noble gesture, it is not always the case. Unless you are one of the fortunate ones, and I am pretty sure there are very few, you can probably recall a time when someone was outright rude about their dismissal of you or someone you know.

OBLIVIOUS TO REJECTION

Not too long ago, while traveling with my husband, I decided to go downstairs to the hotel we were staying at and try their continental breakfast. After grabbing some coffee and one of their muffins, I sat across a group of about a dozen people who were obviously on vacation and excitedly discussed their plans for the day. They had pushed two tables together to make sure everyone had a seat. From what I could gather through their conversation, the large group was made up of about three different families.

I truly enjoy watching people interact with one another in public. When I was a little girl, I often wondered what other people's lives were like in comparison to my own. Nowadays, although I still wonder, my people-watching has more to do with my research and writing on human connections, interactions, and relationships in general. I am always amazed at how people communicate with others, how they carry themselves in situations, and how they express what they seem to be thinking. You can see this through their facial expressions, their posture and body language, the way they dress, or the words they speak.

One of the families in the vacationing group was a husband and wife with two young children: a boy about eight years old and a girl around six. Dad was sitting at the end of the table, participating in the discussion with the other adults, while the young girl wrapped her little arms around his waist. It was apparent she was trying to get his attention. When that didn't do the trick, her arms moved up around his neck. Since she was not quite tall enough to hold dad at his level, she pulled him down towards her, which was clearly an uncomfortable position for the man. As he continued his conversation, he paused for a split second to tell the little girl to stop; quite firmly, I might add. She paid him no mind, and you could see Dad getting frustrated. With her hands still around his neck, the young girl upped the ante and climbed into his lap.

Dad, visibly upset at this point, quite firmly said, "Stop being annoying!" Knowing how powerful words can be, especially at this age, my heart immediately sunk for the little girl.

The boy, who I assumed was the slightly older brother, decided not to be outdone and grabbed Dad, too. At this point, the man had had enough and repeated what he had said earlier to both children this time. "Stop you two, you are being so annoying." He peeled the children off him and ordered them both to sit alone at a different table.

I didn't want to be obvious about my intrusive interest, so I was unsure what type of expression was on the children's faces as they sat apart from the group. I have no idea what the girl felt on the inside when Dad called her annoying, but she did not seem outwardly bothered. Maybe it was because she was attempting to cover her embarrassment in front of the group, or perhaps she was just used to the negative words. What I do know is that she was attempting to get her father's attention, and he rejected her and her attempts with his words and actions.

The scenario does not make him a lousy person. Perhaps he has excellent connections with his children when they are in the comfort of their home. At that moment, however, he was focused on the conversation he was involved in, and the little girl was interrupting his focus. As harsh as his words were, he was more than likely oblivious to the rejection he had just handed his daughter. It appeared that he had no clue how his handling of the situation may have affected the innocent child. This is how a majority of people see their realm. They understand through their eyes and fail to see how their reactions and responses affect those around them.

Trust me, I understand and have witnessed responses from fathers that are undeniably much worse than what this little girl endured while I was observing Some fathers do and say cruel and vile things to their children. Things so awful the child spends years of their adult life unconsciously trying to make sense of it all. Some mothers are in the same boat, I am sure. At different levels, the rejecting words and actions of the parents can potentially destroy a person's life if that person cannot come to grips with these facts: The rejection was about their mom or dad, not them. Therefore, it was beyond their control and unavoidable.

The fact that we live in a world of "me" individuals makes many people unaware of their surroundings. What I mean is that on a day-by-day basis, most people only consider themselves. So, they unintentionally take part in the ego-bruising of people they interact with, whether they are familiar with them or not. It is easy to be so focused on ourselves that we are automatically unaware of others. Most humans' tunnel vision blinds them to the people they encounter daily. And at times, when they do dare to see the rejections' effect on someone else, many brush it off as an overreaction.

REJECTION REALIZED

When I finally received the call back from my dream job interviewer, the message on the other end of the phone threw me for a loop. I was excited and had anxiously been waiting for this moment, but my enthusiasm was short-lived. In my heart, I believed the job was mine. I sat and listened in a state of shock for what seemed like an eternity. Instead of giving me a start date so that I could put in my two weeks' notice at my current job, which felt like a paid prison, the voice said something totally different. "We regret to inform you that we have decided to go with someone else."

"What? You have got to be kidding me," I thought. The optimistic scenario I had played in my head for the past week had been shattered.

I was completely crushed. The voice on the other end did not stop there, however. Maybe they thought digging the blade of disapproval just slightly deeper by explaining why someone else got my dream job was a good idea. In a very matter-of-fact tone, she told me that their new employee was a very experienced driver with the license I had been studying for nonstop. That license was supposed to make the job mine. In other words, my skillset was not up to par, making me less qualified. There was so much I wanted to say, to ask, but nothing came out of my mouth. I have to admit I took the news pretty hard and quite personally. My expectations were high, and I was absolutely let down.

Anyone familiar with the sting of rejection can guess what happened next. The voices in my head started. You know those voices, the ones that fill you with doubt and self-deprecating thoughts about who you are as a person. They are the voices that tend to paralyze you with fear and make you second-guess your next steps . . . every single one of your next steps.

It is vital to note that the harder the rejection hits, the louder the voices become. Add this to the fact that if you have been contaminated in the past by rejection, the negativity from the experience will appear much more magnified.

YOU ARE NOT THE ONE

The reality, however, was not that the hiring manager made a conscious decision to vote against me. Truth be told, she barely knew me. This person based their ruling on their individual goal. Which, believe it or not, had nothing to do with helping me land my dream job. She had to fulfill the obligation of her responsibilities, and it had zero to do with me. Her charge was simply to hire the person best suited for the position. Sadly, that day, I was not the one. My perfect record for scoring the jobs I had applied for was ruined.

Back in those days, I did not know any better, so of course, the aftershock of it all sent me into a swell of self-pity and uncertainties about my competencies. Looking back, that hiring manager was not as callous as I would like you to believe, but she certainly was unaware of how negatively her call impacted me. In her mind, it was not a rejection of me but instead a welcoming of someone else. The "someone else" was helping to fulfill her very own obligations to her boss.

Through my eyes, paired with the words in the dictionary, hiring someone other than me meant I was inadequate because I had somehow failed to meet another person's needs. And while the disappointment of my "dream job" is on the bottom rung of the ladder of all the rejections I have faced throughout my life, at the end of the day, it was still a rejection.

This outcome and the internal struggle around it are shared by people each and every day. The unfortunate reality is that for many more, the agony comes from more severe strikes than a simple job loss. It comes from people who were supposed to love us and protect us. Maybe through acts of neglect, abandonment, mistreatment, and all horrendous kinds of abuse. The memories are deep-rooted scars in the heart and serve as constant torment for countless individuals. The raw truth is that unless you are open to becoming a hermit or finding another way to cut all ties with humanity, there is no avoiding it. Rejection is, without a doubt, unavoidable.

"We are hard pressed on all sides, but not crushed; perplexed, but not in despair; persecuted, but not forsaken; struck down, but not destroyed."

2 CORINTHIANS 4:8-9

CHAPTER THREE

IT DISRUPTS LIFE-GIVING CONNECTIONS

"Connection is why we're here. We are hardwired to connect with others; it's what gives purpose and meaning to our lives, and without it, there is suffering."

BRENE BROWN

Consider the interactions you have with other people in your life. Certainly, there are those who you are closer to than others. If you are like most, the sting of disregard is often felt deeper the closer you are to the disregarder. However, despite the closeness or lack thereof, you would agree that it is unlikely to find a more dreadful feeling in the world than that of being snubbed.

It may come from an act of disrespect or a simple cold shoulder. It matters not who rebuffs us; the sense that derives from the idea that we are unwanted or unwelcomed causes a feeling of disregard, discomfort, and, in some, defensiveness, at the very least. We may not realize what we are experiencing internally at the moment.

Certain scenarios could bring back memories. Perhaps being the last one picked for the fourth-grade kickball team by the kids in the class comes up when you are excluded from lunch with a group of colleagues. You might be reminded of the parent who constantly ignored you as a child when your suggestion was discounted at a work meeting. Either way, the same feelings of offense and hurt will likely well up inside many of us at some intensity. Usually, the level is higher than we anticipated.

The mystery behind such emotional indignation is quite simple, actually. We were made for relationship. As human beings, we were meant to be social. There is an innate desire to connect with one another, to belong, and to be known inside all of us.

In the Hebrew Bible, this truth originates with our Creator in the Garden of Eden. God formed Adam, and shortly after that, He noted that it was "not good for man to be alone," so He created Eve. She is described as a suitable mate for him (Genesis 2:18). While it is true that Adam had God, and that would have been enough for him, the Creator addressed the part in the human soul of man (and woman) that would flourish when a connection was made with another earthly individual. This yearning is a gift from God.

CONNECTION IN THE MIRACLE OF LIFE

For those of you less moved by religion, let us look at it through a different lens. The science behind the miracle of life begins with connection. A man's seed joins (*connects*) together with a woman's mature egg, forming a zygote. This single cell now contains all the information it needs to create a fetus: a complete set of chromosomes, 23 from the mother and 23 from the father. As the zygote travels toward the woman's uterus, the mother's body nourishes it. When it arrives at its destination, it attaches (*connects*) to the womb and is now ready to develop into an embryo.

As this miracle of life continues growing, it establishes links (*connections*) with the mother's blood supply, forming the placenta. While the baby continues to develop, the umbilical cord implants (*connects*) into the placenta, taking blood back and forth between mother and baby. Through the (*connected*) cord, many miracles continue to take place. The unborn child is receiving nourishment, oxygen, and other support needed to survive while also eliminating wastes and carbon dioxide that could harm the baby through the mother's circulatory system. This beautiful connection is indeed a miracle.

In the final stage of birth, as the baby enters the world, he is still attached (*connected*) to his mother. If there are no complications, he will be placed on her chest, providing skin-to-skin contact (*connection*) for the first time. Immediately after, the cord, once the center of life for the unborn child, is clamped and then cut. And although the baby has been separated from his former life supply and is now breathing on his own, he is now in his mother's arms (*connecting*). In a brand-new phase of life for both mom and child, the connection made between the two will determine a great deal of his future. If it is solid and built on love, his future holds great potential, but if it is broken or worn out by rejection, the possibility of impending suffering is quite certain.

BROKEN CONNECTIONS CAUSE PAIN IN THE BRAIN

Consider the loss of connection through the world of technology. There is a global demand for the miracle of Wi-Fi, which connects us in an instant. This unseen force powers the world through the access of emails, web browsing, television binge-watching, and countless other forms of information and entertainment. Depending on the moment and the individual, there are those who will go into a fit of panic without this tool. The truth is some people will go to great lengths to ensure they have the best connection possible. The loss of signal causes the vicarious world many live through their devices to simply cease. Although there could be several reasons for the disruption, when tablets, computers, T.V.s and phones abruptly disconnect, it causes incredible frustration and agitation for the masses. The agony of interruption, however superficial, causes certain people to pay ridiculous amounts of money to gain, regain, or keep their signal connection strong.

Similarly, but on a much more serious level, studies prove time and again that if people are connected directly to another person, in some type of personal relationship, and the connection suddenly goes missing or is disrupted for too long, there is discomfort and pain. Not only that, but in some cases, there is also an implication of psychological effects such as hopelessness, despair, and depression. If you have ever had your heart broken by an unexpected breakup, a betrayal, a divorce, or the loss of a loved one, the disconnection has undoubtedly given you the experience of some of these effects.

The importance of the necessity for connection is confirmed through the field of neuroscience, the study of the brain, which testifies to the fact that we are indeed social beings in need of connecting to others. Neuroscientists predominately focus on the structure and function of the brain. Although the discoveries have been numerous, the human brain is so complex that even after centuries of study and research, experts still have many unanswered questions. However, evidence of this human wiring comes from a correlation discovered between social and physical pain in the brain when human connection is fragmented or broken.

An article in *Scientific American* explains that the data in a study of mammals ranging from mice to men indicates immense suffering when the severing of a social bond occurs. In other words, if you pull a child away from its mother, intentionally or not, a type of anguish happens in the brain. No matter the species, the need for connection is perhaps as critical as our need for food.

As humans, the pain caused by rejection is very real. Just like physical pain, the brain reacts to emotional pain, whether we realize it or not. A study of the brain led by a team at the University of Michigan Medical School showed that the natural opioid released to relieve physical pain in an individual was also the same released in participants experiencing rejection.

Perhaps more astounding was the fact that certain individuals released more of this pain-inhibiting chemical in response to rejection than others. These people appeared better prepared to deal with the effects of being disregarded and seemed to just move on. On the other hand, those releasing fewer amounts of the opioid had a more difficult time dealing with the rejection. These people are likely to find a way to develop their own defense mechanisms. It is highly probable the coping strategies they come up with will lead to future deliberate disconnections from others.

Individuals who choose to spend long periods of time alone may want to disagree with this truth. Yet, even the most recluse people will likely suffer in the hands of an unwarranted disconnection. It pains the soul, no matter how tough we want to claim to be. In fact, many of these callous one-(wo)man shows are developed because of a painful past disconnection. More than likely, their self-erected wall is an invisible protection against any imminent possibility of disregard.

My guess is that at some point, this individual who was created for connection faced a rejection of sorts. The multitude of confusing emotions that followed was distressing enough for the person to consciously or subconsciously make a way to avoid future rejections. After all, humanity possesses a natural ability to generate self-defense mechanisms subconsciously. Unbeknownst to them, they claim this is just how they were born.

Furthermore, studies show that one of the biggest culprits to brain decline among people of all ages is when people disconnect or feel disconnected from other people. This disengagement is why it is believed so many retirees begin to deteriorate. The sudden isolation from people they have been connected to for years, if not decades, is so detrimental it tends to shorten a person's life span. Some studies claim that people can lose up to fifteen years of life without a sense of community.

On the other hand, if the same person decides to volunteer for a couple of years after their retirement, actual brain growth takes place in the hippocampus. This area plays a vital role in forming, organizing, and storing memories. Grandparents who decide to spend time with or care for their grandchildren in their newfound spare time tend to live longer than those who spend those years alone.

EARLY DISCONNECTIONS CAN AFFECT FUTURE BRAIN CONNECTIONS

A three-year study done in Japan on adults 65 and older highlights that the damage done in childhood disconnection can carry over into the latter years. According to the Japan Gerontological Evaluation Study research, the more trauma incidents a child experienced, the more likely they were to develop dementia in their older age. With over 10 million new cases of the disease every year, it is worth looking into its ties with rejection.

Aside from having the longest life span, the group of Japanese individuals they analyzed also had parents who went through World War II. One-fifth of this group of adults lost their parents to that war while they were young children. Of course, the loss of a parent immediately causes a vital connection to be broken in the life of a child. While this is not meant to be equated with deliberate abandonment, the probability of a child with one or no parents facing future rejection through abuse or neglect is very high and almost unavoidable. The study's findings showed that those with three or more traumatic experiences, such as parental death, divorce, family violence, physical and psychological abuse, or neglect, were associated with increased dementia risks.

Other schools of thought indicate early childhood disconnection through trauma will also upset other areas of a person's health. We will delve further into this topic in the following section of this book, *The Toxicity of Rejection*. For the moment, however, the findings in this study suggest all the poisonous forms of rejection in the earlier life of the participants pushed them into a probable loss of future connection with their own minds. While this is a very recent study, and one of the very few on the dementia link, I do regrettably have personal insight on the issue and tend to agree with the high likelihood of the study's findings.

DISCONNECTIONS, BAD CONNECTIONS, AND DEMENTIA

As I pen these words, I sit and reminisce about my precious mother, who recently passed away after a long battle with dementia. She was laid to rest the day before her seventy-second birthday. The era she was born into and the people around her were less than kind to Mom. Although I will share more of her story in upcoming chapters, for the purposes of this topic, it is essential to mention how life began for her.

She was abandoned by her birth father shortly after she was born. I clearly remember the trip we made as a family to meet him for the first and last time, I might add. A photo commemorates the visit, and while she attempted to make amends with him somewhere in her early thirties, the relationship did not go anywhere. The wife of one of her half-brothers reached back out to her through a letter, but her birth father made no such effort. At least not that I was aware of. I can imagine it added to the initial pain she held in her heart since she never spoke much of her long-lost family again.

My parents had been together for almost forty-five years when Mom was diagnosed with FTD. Frontotemporal dementia is a nasty neurocognitive disorder that affects the lobes in the brain, causing dramatic changes in language, behavior, and personality, all the attributes that make us human. It is a rare form of dementia, with no cure and an average life course of 6 to 8 years. At the young age of sixty, this horrific disease began to slowly steal away our mother.

Over the course of a few years, Mom lost her memory, which affected her ability to communicate. That, of course, was followed by a disconnection to the people that once meant everything to her. In the beginning stages, she often forgot who we were. Still, perhaps the hardest thing to experience was the aggressive outbursts of words and profanities she would unexpectedly hurl at her beloved babies.

At times, it seemed that those she held closest to her heart when she was of sound mind took the greatest hits. While we all understood that this was one of the dominating behaviors that came with FTD, it still was disheartening to be on the receiving end. After all, we were having to deal with the disconnection of the mother we previously knew. The loving woman who once doted on her children was now effortlessly infuriated at their very presence. Watching her deteriorate was, of course, hard on all of us, but the implications of Mom's visible worsening were on a different level for my dad.

Growing up, our home was very far from perfect. Although we never wanted for anything, there always seemed to be some sort of drama around the corner. To start, Mom and Dad grew up in very dysfunctional homes. Our parents loved each other, but because they were both headstrong and carried so much toxic baggage from their upbringing, the harmony came in spurts, quickly disrupted by petty yet fiery disagreements. Peace was short-lived in our home, and we never knew when the dam would break between the two.

One thing was certain; Mom was the center of the universe for us all. As a housewife, her entire life revolved around tending to her husband and caring for her children. Our home was immaculate; we never missed a meal, and she ensured we were always well-dressed and clean. Needless to say, when we got the news that she was sick, we knew it was our turn to pay back the favor. And we did everything in our power to do right by her.

After about four years into the battle with dementia, we realized it had become too dangerous to leave Mom home alone. My brother and sisters all put in as much time as each was able. My baby sister spent countless days keeping Mom company in the earlier years until it was time for her to return to work. I was thankful to be able to take some time off to spend with her as well. When Dad's retirement date came up, he took it as a sign that it was his turn to stay home with her. This turned out to be much more challenging than he had anticipated.

If you have ever lived with or cared for a loved one with dementia, you can testify to the suffering it brings to all the parties involved. Watching the able body and sound mind of the person you once knew slowly disintegrate right before your eyes is beyond heartbreaking. It does not happen all at once, either, which is harder to deal with in many ways. Some recognize the soul-stealing disease as the "long good-bye," which makes total sense. The grief seems to span through the duration of the disease because every day, you lose a little bit more of your loved one, and other than trying to keep them comfortable, there really is not much one can do.

Around the ninth year and in the final stages of the horrendous disease, we started questioning whether the time had come for us to transition Mom into a twenty-four-hour Memory Care unit. Although we all did our best to fill in the gaps, with my brother, sisters, and I stopping by to help out, it was taking a toll on my father, who, at that point, was her main caretaker. Dad would not have it. He was fighting hard against Mom's emotional withdrawal from him, so the thought of moving her was just too much to bear. Having lived the majority of his life with her, it was perfectly understandable. This made any conversation around transferring Mom into a memory care nursing unit a sore subject for Dad. The tough, unemotional guy we knew growing up broke down in tears at the thought of losing that last bit of connection he had with his wife of almost fifty years, albeit only physically.

While there is no hard evidence to conclude that Mom's early encounter with rejection guaranteed her tragic meeting with dementia, the Japan Gerontological Evaluation Study research makes the possibility extremely plausible. At the very least, if the science is correct, the rejection by her birth father may well have played a role in laying the groundwork for the start of the disconnection in her mind. As you will see later, this was unfortunately not the last rejection that Mom encountered throughout her life.

REJECTION AND DISSOCIATION

Ironically, dementia comes with many parallels similar to rejection, such as changes in mood, volatile reactions, loss of conversation, and loss of interest in things and people. Although the patient is unaware of their actions, they unknowingly mimic rejection's negative effects. All of this was new and shocking to us.

While I cannot speak for my brother and sisters, in the beginning, Mom's unintentional dismissal of us activated an emotional disconnection inside of me towards her. It sounds callous, but allow me to explain.

It is common for individuals who have a history of repetitive trauma to have an attribute of dissociation. Dissociation is a type of emotional disconnection, with different ranges starting with normal daydreaming all the way to a blackout state. Science indicates that everyone uses this defense occasionally to protect themselves from various traumas based on their fight-or-flight responses to perceived threats. For me, it was a natural coping mechanism that I had subconsciously picked up in my early years to deal with distressing events.

Consider dissociation something like a safety switch in the brain. When something hurtful, tough or scary happens it automatically kicks in and disconnects the person from the situation to help them deal with being overwhelmed. It is comparable to a pause button on your emotions, and at times, your memories as well.

Our childhood was plagued with many emotional peaks and valleys brought on by the perpetual clashing and arguing of parental personalities. Although I did not realize it back then, when things got chaotic in my home, I learned to disconnect myself emotionally from my surroundings. It created somewhat of a numbing effect that helped avoid, or at the very least reduce, the tension that rose inside me when my parents were fighting.

The developing minds of children use it to cope with disturbing emotions or memories they find difficult to process or handle. It could also come from witnessing an accident, bullying, neglect, loss, and grief. If a child's dissociative experience is severe or repetitive, they can carry these tendencies into adulthood. Some cases are so extreme that the child may develop what is known as a dissociative disorder, a loss of reality, where they can experience interference of consciousness, memory, identity, or the way they perceive the world.

It is important to note that there is an entire population that unknowingly walks around at some level dissociated from life. This disconnection is not always easy to spot since a person can work at a job, raise children, and serve in their community or church, all disguised as busyness. Eventually, it will catch up and create issues.

It was an involuntary escape route in my childhood, so I did not have to focus on what was happening around me. Although it served as a form of protection while growing up, it was my go-to defense later in life. The switch would automatically turn on during moments of stress, even though I was oblivious to it. Needless to say, it produced plenty of relationship issues for me that could have been avoided.

Later in life, in a much safer and healthier state of mind, and through a long process of healing, I was able to recognize the patterns leading to the disconnect. Instead of putting up a wall so that I could avoid the issue, the feelings, and the people involved, I learned how to stay put in the moment, pay attention to what I was feeling and not take things personally. As an alternative to automatically reacting, I learned how to respond by honing in on where the feelings were coming from. At the end of the day, there is power in taking responsibility for my own emotions. The switch has now became more of a super-power than a survival shield. I have especially found it to be beneficial when I am under duress and need a resolution to a situation without being bombarded with the emotional attachments.

In Mom's case, because I felt we were up against a wall and needed to move quickly, it served me well. We all put our heads together, made some calls and prayed. Right on time, God opened doors and moved mountains for us. Before we knew it, we had the resources we needed for a full-time caretaker. This took a massive load off of my father and made it possible for Mom to stay at home where she could be kept comfortable. As far as the caretaker was concerned, we struck gold and could not have asked for a better person. Marie, Mom's primary nurse, treated her with the ultimate respect and dignity. She was such a blessing to all of us.

This horrible mind-stealing illness substantially reduced Mom's ability to connect with us. But, although the evidence shows that the trauma of her youth may have contributed to the disconnection from her mind, there is also research that points to the fact that the connection with those who loved her in her latter years likely helped

A 1979 landmark study demonstrated that individuals who had strong social connections decreased their chances of mortality by three times compared to those who were less connected to others. My mother lived well into her twelfth year of battle with a disease that generally allows a person to live only half of that time. I strongly believe through God's grace and strength, our love and determination to keep the connection going on our end, sustained her longer than many thought would be possible. This is proof to me that connection is crucial to our existence.

INTERRUPTED CONNECTIONS

We all can attest to the fact that we grow closer to the people we spend the most time with. Understandably, strong connections that are solidified over long periods of time experience great pain after a separation occurs, and of course, that makes sense in the natural. The death of a spouse is so devastating it is recognized as the most stressful event in a person's life. Whether the marriage was strong or filled with chaos, the emotional chemistry that created their connection has been broken.

If you do a quick internet search, you can find stories of elderly couples married for decades, dying months, and some even days apart. It turns out the distress caused by the disconnection, if sudden and severe enough, can produce ailments that can lead to the surviving spouse's death. This is known as broken heart syndrome or stress-induced cardiomyopathy in the cardiological field. Although it occurs more often in the elderly, it can happen at any age from a surge of stress due to a divorce, separation, betrayal, or rejection.

This is just more proof that our human makeup requires connection. The length of the relationship does not matter when it goes missing or is disrupted. This can be demonstrated by the simple observation of a newborn baby. Obviously, without the human intervention of providing essentials, such as food, water and basic care, the child will not survive. On the other hand, when this intervention takes place, and a healthy connection is built with the child based around love and security, a formula for resilience becomes the foundation for a thriving, self-confident adult later in life.

Unfortunately, this is not always the norm. Although the tangibles, such as food and water, are not likely to be withheld from a baby, the emotional connection we were wired for is often overlooked. Everyone knows a tiny, helpless newborn needs to be fed and changed regularly, but the same cannot be said for the child's natural longing to be loved. While parents often want nothing more than to embrace and pour affection on their newborn, the fact that it is as essential as being fed eludes many.

A fair warning: this next part may be a bit tough to hear, and many of us can probably relate. I know I can.

An extremely busy and well-intentioned working mom or dad will devise a meticulous plan for their baby's care while they work. They ensure the caregiver is more than qualified to ensure they are well cared for. No harm done, right? While I wish I could tell you otherwise, there is evidence to the contrary. The parent may have great intentions, but that does not matter. As far as the baby is concerned, mom or dad left them behind with a stranger for most of the day.

This is a rather challenging situation in today's economy. The alternative of not working and staying home to raise a child until they are more secure is nearly impossible for most families. While going to work is often in the household's best interest, it does not change what happens to a child's emotions in the midst of it.

Likewise, a husband who thinks his only job is to be a provider of food and a home for his family sends a similar message to his wife. The point is that the husband simply does what he believes best. Unlike the baby, the wife can reason, yet she still feels the disconnect. In both cases, a lack of awareness will create an emotional divide. The seeds of rejection have been planted. The extent of how those seeds grow is determined by the child's resiliency level. Ironically, this depends on their prior parental connection. How the parents fill in those gaps when they are not busy with work can make all the difference as they grow.

CHILDHOOD CONNECTION PATTERNS REPEATED

In some instances, this denied love and affection is from an unhealthy parent repeating the cycle of disconnection they experienced in their own life. Mildly put, they themselves had horrible role models. Again, the reason matters little to the innocent infant. In the field of psychology there is much credence given to the idea that human connection, or a lack thereof, in a person's childhood, produces specific definitive outcomes. When the basic needs for parental love, direction, affection and safety go unmet during the first years of life, it tends to cause deficits in the latter years. It is a form of rejection in the young child's mind.

Take home where the parent or parents are extremely busy. They simply want to do their very best to materially provide what they did not have themselves growing up for their child and naïvely overlook the importance of connection. Whatever the case, it usually will carry over into their personal relationships when they are grown. Many children subconsciously conclude something is wrong with them, whether the child's parent was terribly toxic or just naïve.

Without getting into the dynamics of all that occurs in the soul of a child who does not have this critical need met, I will venture to address this one simple truth. There is an unseen but obvious wound left where a parental connection failed, often innocently. The substance of the parent-child relationship is grounded on the emotional connection. When that is left out of the mix, at higher levels especially, it molds adults into joyless and disconnected people.

This has led to a society filled with grown individuals overwhelmed by a myriad of confusing emotions. Some of these groups sense something is not quite right inside them but cannot seem to put their finger on it. They unknowingly walk around with a wounded soul, trying to satiate the unfilled place. The results can be seen throughout their life. They make poor choices, form unhealthy relationships, take up harmful behaviors, and ultimately feel a lack of self-worth.

If you constantly feel stressed, lonely, lost, confused, hopeless, or even inadequate, but you are not sure why, perhaps examining your childhood a bit closer will bring you some long-awaited answers. It could go beyond simply feeling distant in a home with busy parents.

You may have memories of a good childhood, doing well in school with a caring mom and dad. You were rarely, if ever, physically punished. Your parents may have been well-intentioned, always being sure to take care of your physical needs. Yet you grew up in a home where your expression of feelings was either ignored or diminished. Perhaps not intentionally, but because they battled daily chaos in their own life, repeating what was lived out in front of them as children. Maybe it was just saying things that were said to them. The old cliché of telling a child to stop crying or you will give them something to cry about is popular but very detrimental to the innocent young mind trying to make sense of their emotions.

This is not a championing for the progression of an excessively sensitive generation. I do not believe parents should have to walk on eggshells in the presence of their children, constantly going overboard to protect their feelings.

My children were loved, but I seldom went in to rescue them from their choices. They were raised on the belief that making mistakes and learning from them was never really a mistake. However, like most parents, hindsight is twenty-twenty, and there was a lot about parenting I missed the mark on. I do look back now and second-guess myself. Like most, I could have done a better job. There are words that I spoke that I wish I could take back and different actions I wish I would have taken. If I had a do-over, I would have worked less and spent more time with them. However, no matter our regrets, we cannot change the past. The only way to redeem our mistakes is by making the future better through what we have learned. Maybe my shortcomings will serve you in some way.

I can give credibility to the fact that many people who walk around in a fog, with a sense of sadness, an emptiness, even when everything around them seems to be going well, feel like something is missing. Since both science and the Scriptures demonstrate how connection is woven into the very fiber of our being, it makes sense that the pain suffered when that vital connection is broken may likely be the reason.

"Let each of you look not only to his own interests but also to the interests of others."

PHILIPPIANS 2:4 (ESV)

CHAPTER FOUR

IT HITS AT DIFFERENT INTENSITIES

"Sometimes I feel my whole life has been one big rejection."

MARILYN MONROE

Middle school memories are usually jammed with ruthless recollections of rejection. At least, that was the case for me in my very early pre-teen years. According to experts, 99 percent of the population feels the same way, so I am not alone in the personal perspective I held during these very tough times. You may have an unpleasant memory or two of your own branded into your mind.

At this age, the delusion that all eyes are on you, judging your every move, can be pretty distressing. Building the perfect image in an effort to fit in takes front and center in the lives of most twelve- and thirteen-year-old children entering this gauntlet of social pressure for the first time in their lives. For the majority of them, status in the group is everything. During this period, most children encounter a deep sense of rejection brought on by the fallacy that the spotlight of judgment is always on them.

In the late 1960s, the term *imaginary audience* was coined by David Elkind as he researched and worked to describe the adolescent's ego and their assumption that they were the object of everyone else's total focus. It is no different today in the twenty-first century. Think of any kid you know entering puberty, and you have probably witnessed, more often than not, an outburst of panic over something seemingly insignificant. These expressive overreactions leave adults wondering what just happened. Aside from the hormones and emotional immaturity, you can blame their magnified imagination for this season in their life.

Perhaps you have found yourself shaking your head and wondering why you see so many in this age group walking around wearing oversized, heavy hoodies in 90-degree weather. Some will argue against this, but the imaginary audience is quite likely the reason.

At age twelve, my security blanket came in the form of a red hooded Immokalee Indian nylon windbreaker. Growing up in the sweltering sunny state of Florida, I rarely, if ever, left home without it that seventh-grade year. I even came up with a brilliant solution when the heat got the best of me; I would keep it on until I could not stand it any longer, and then I would just take it off and tie it around my waist. It was the perfect protection against unwanted attention, no matter how unreal it was. Like today's youth, I used it as a tangible shield covering my insecurities and guarding myself against ridicule and rejection.

While I am sure some will insist this piece of clothing is a fashion statement, the fact is for most, it provides them safety from the perceived scrutiny of the crowd. Teens and preteens are going through immense changes in their bodies, making them so self-conscious about what is happening to them they believe that their peers and even total strangers are constantly watching and scrutinizing everything they say and everything they do. Tie that to the ones who live in homes filled with dysfunction and have already endured several stints of rejection. This means just a slight hint of disapproval from someone can wreak mental havoc on a preteen.

Of course, there are homes where teens get great support and encouragement during these times. This does not mean the struggles are eliminated; it just means that the negative effects of what they believe to be condemnation are at a lower level and, more than likely, short-lived.

EVERYONE IS LOOKING AT ME

Now, unless we personally connect with this time in our life or intentionally empathize with this age group and all the alarming newness they face, we will disregard the "reality of their imaginary audience" as simply dramatics. As foreign as the behaviors of the adolescent may be to us, they can explain the different levels of rejection people experience. Taking into account that what appears to be a ridiculous overaction in our eyes is a very legitimate reaction for them.

Perhaps, most peculiar is that Elkind's research presupposed that the imaginary audience dwindles as the young person gets older, eventually disappearing altogether somewhere in adulthood. However, in my world of counseling and coaching, I would have to say this is not always the case, especially with individuals who have past rejection issues. Spending a significant amount of time in real, deep discussions with people of all ages who are trying to get their lives together, I have encountered a majority of individuals who were consumed and controlled by what they believed was someone else's negative view of them. In each case, the perspective of the wounded individual determined the intensity of the perceived rejection.

My point is that it is clear some people never quite outgrow their imaginary audience, no matter their age. They have a sense, whether they realize it or not, that the world of others revolves around them. An unanswered text from a busy friend turns into a "what did I do wrong" deliberation in their head. It is as if these people are expecting rejection to happen. You will find that they tend to get the wrong idea about and overreact to the words or actions of others. Their personality can range from highly aggressive to painfully passive.

For example, the former will take great offense if they ask someone for a favor and are turned down. Granted, no one likes to be told no, but these individuals will take it to the extreme by lashing out at an unsuspecting naysayer at a later time. They seem to record the rejection in their memory and wait for the perfect time to "pay" the other person back. They are very suspicious, so they may constantly accuse their significant other of cheating on them with no factual basis.

Those who are more passive tend to go out of their way to ensure they are accepted and liked. This is dangerous for many women and men who find themselves in toxic relationships. Instead of walking away and doing what is best for them, they will go to extreme, nonsensical measures to get their partner into their good graces.

Never having learned coping skills, these individuals experience great difficulty with trivial matters. If you add neglect and emotional, physical, or sexual abuse to the wide range of issues endured throughout their childhood, a slight rebuff from someone can create a sort of devastation in their eyes. On the other hand, if you slight one of the luckier ones, those who received support from their family and suffered much less hardship, they will simply brush it off. Consequently, you now have different perceived levels of rejection.

REJECTION AT EVERY LEVEL

The seemingly insignificant types of rejection in life are no big deal to most of us, especially if we are the ones doing the rejecting. On the surface level and just to lighten the mood on this ominous topic, let us look at it through the example of food. If we go with the Cambridge Dictionary definition, the act of refusing to accept something, saying no to a dish of some sort that someone offers us, is considered a rejection. Turning down an extra piece of cake at a party does little harm and, in fact, is probably beneficial for us all from time to time. Although it is a silly example, it is meant to shine a light on the different rejection levels around us and see how easy it is to participate. Turning down a gift or an invitation can possibly, at the very least, hurt someone's feelings and put a slight strain on the relationship with the inviter or the gift giver. But most people do not give it a second thought and quickly let it roll off their back. Again, we reject things we do not want and barely notice.

However, it is a whole other story when we are on the receiving end of being dismissed. The rejection looks and feels completely different. Think about the last time you felt the sting. Was it subtle or blatantly overt? The former may have caused us to question ourselves momentarily, or perhaps it created a fog of confusion in our head for hours or even days.

Maybe you run into someone you have not seen in a while, someone you felt you clicked with before. A mild sense of excitement rises up inside you when your eyes meet. However, instead of reciprocating the enthusiasm, they barely react, acting as if they hardly know you. It may wound you momentarily. You may even play out the situation in your head for a few hours, trying to figure out their reaction. Perhaps you even find yourself wondering what you did wrong. After a day or so, for most of us, life would go on.

A harsher rejection, one that no one can deny happened, such as abuse, alienation, bullying, or betrayal, has effects that are multiplied many times over. Depending on the state of mind of the recipient, it can bring with it the possibility of additional cutting consequences. The impact can be so profound that the pain endured from it changes the person in a way that their entire life is now veiled by the hurt it birthed. The decisions a person makes, their reactions to even the most minor offenses, and even the compliments received are seen through the tainted lens of this type of rejection.

Although rejection is, at the very least, uncomfortable at almost all levels, it is easy to see the noticeable difference when it involves the human heart. It goes beyond just hurt feelings. Especially if the rejection is ongoing and, in particular, comes from a familial relationship such as someone we love, trust, and respect. For example, if you have never known your father, you felt disconnected from your mother, or perhaps your marriage ended in divorce after discovering your spouse was having an affair, you most assuredly experienced the pain of rejection at a much deeper level. You held an idea or belief that expected the offender to meet a need or fill a responsibility in your life, and that expectation was utterly destroyed. In turn, it almost certainly damaged something inside of you.

In these types of situations, at least one person builds their part of the relationship on trust, a vital ingredient in any close connection. When that trust is broken, the wounded individual feels a great sense of betrayal, amongst various other painful emotions. Many feel as if their entire life has been shattered. The distinction here arises from deep damage to the human soul. This type of pain is so seemingly irreparable it paints the way a person sees their entire world. Always looking at life and others through this corrupted angle.

To fully grasp the varying rejection levels, we must first take a closer view of its meaning. Merriam-Webster has a lot to say about the word "rejecting." As a verb, it is the action of refusing to accept, to cast off; throwback, or spew out. In layman's terms, you may simply use the phrase "unwanted." If we are talking about passing up dessert at a dinner party or returning a Christmas gift that you would have never purchased for yourself, there is no harm done. Unless you run into your gift giver in the customer service line at the department store, and they catch you in the act. The scenario of getting caught getting a refund for the unwanted item has the potential to cause the offense level to go up a notch or two, depending on who you are dealing with. While the example may seem ridiculous, the point is that a distraught victim of repeated rejection would likely be very offended in this case. The intensity of the rejection they experience will likely be high.

Granted, my experience of losing my dream job, although traumatic to me at the time, is on a shallower level when it comes to the range in the levels of rejection we all have come to endure. However, an individual with a trail of rejections already recorded in their soul, something seemingly minor to most people, could hit at a much deeper level and send this person on an emotional downward spiral.

EXPECTATIONS UP THE PAIN ANTE

Mother Teresa said, "The world's greatest tragedy is unwantedness; the world's greatest disease is loneliness." This selfless soul spent her days in orphanages serving many of the unforgotten in the land. Although she witnessed firsthand the heartbreak of disease and hunger, she believed that those who were unloved suffered the worst type of tragedy. The loneliness that came from being discarded was crippling for the children of Calcutta, as it would be for anyone who feels they have been thrown away by those who were meant to care for them the most.

Abandonment, a clear form of rejection, hurts no matter who the perpetrator may be. In a perfect world, the last person one expects to be abandoned by is a parent. From a scriptural perspective, Dads are to provide protection and be an earthly representation of God's love and leadership for the child. If chosen correctly, his words can be a powerful inspiration for the youngster's future. Moms, on that same note, are indebted to nurture the child. It is their ability to comfort that teaches the children to deal with pain, whether it be from a physical fall or a friend's rebuff. The part parents play in life is absolutely significant.

Realistically speaking, we do not live in a perfect world, so moms and dads are bound to make mistakes. If they are anything like me, they can probably look back at how they raised a child or their children and see areas they would do differently if given the opportunity.

LEVELS OF LONELINESS

The disconnection, or feeling of disconnection with people, while uncomfortable and lonely, often comes from an unmet expectation. We innocently anticipated something from someone that did not come to fruition. Usually, the more attached we are to a person, the higher the expectation, and the greater the disappointment will be. When the unmet expectations are perceived as a rejection, a sense of loneliness can begin to take over. The irony is that past rejections can implore people to detach themselves from others in an effort to avoid future rejections. This only exasperates the sense of loneliness.

A quick internet search reveals loneliness is the state of being alone, being cut off from others, and feeling sad or empty because of it. It is, however, quite a subjective emotion since some people enjoy their own company, whereas others can feel alone in a crowded room. This means the emotion sets in when a person believes they do not have a choice. Typically, the feeling of loneliness is temporary for most people.

Let me note something important before we explore this further. The disease of loneliness comes in more than one form, and there are serious instances where it can lead to a deterioration in one's mental health. *Situational loneliness* is birthed out of changes that cause a person to feel isolated, such as a big move, a divorce, or someone struggling with singleness. The period of isolation during the COVID-19 shutdown created a condition for this type of loneliness in people's lives globally. However, situational loneliness is easily resolvable. Connecting with the right people or receiving short-term counseling can alleviate feelings of hopelessness.

Emotional loneliness derives from the lack of relationships or attachments. Perhaps you need someone to talk to, but do not feel connected to anyone. A married person can feel lonely due to a disconnection with their spouse. You may have spotted the couple sitting in a restaurant, both staring off into space, looking like they would rather be anywhere else but with their partner. Maybe it's as simple as a disagreement or as complex as a deliberate detachment. Either way, both are generally associated with unmet expectations and quite likely include elevated feelings of rejection by one or both parties. Couple therapy, or at the very least a heart-to-heart conversation, would be quite helpful in bringing relief to this type of loneliness.

The most severe type is *chronic loneliness*. It means what it says. It is a lingering loneliness that does not seem to subside. There is a constant feeling of being alone, even when people are all around. This person does not seem to possess the ability to connect with others at a deeper level. It often comes from an internal struggle. Related to deep-seated issues such as trauma or abuse, the loneliness occurs more from the pain of unresolved hurt. While past rejection may be the culprit for this type of loneliness, even when expectations are met, there seems to be no relief for the emptiness. Usually paired with depression and, at times, suicidal ideation, it is often clinical in nature and requires a great deal of inner healing. Professional and spiritual help should be sought immediately.

Professional counseling can also serve situational and emotional loneliness well, but they are not usually as serious. They come about from pondering on unmet expectations. In our mind, consciously or unconsciously, we expect a certain reaction or response from an individual. Most of us grow up having some idea of how people should act or react to us. If we are pretty levelheaded, we expect good service at a restaurant, we expect our children to respect us, our friends to be there when we need them, and we expect our spouses to be faithful. None of these expectations are irrational.

Unfortunately, we live in a fallen world, and people will disappoint us. Ironically, the closer we are to the person who has somehow let us down, the deeper the hurt will be felt. The more profound the wound, the further out the negative wave of impact travels, and the more it will affect our lives.

REJECTION INTENSIFIED

If the waitress at the local Perkins snubs us, it is simple. We can just give it right back to her, in our defense. Sure, maybe we will get upset, but once we regain our composure, we can either complain to the manager or simply withhold her tip (I used to be a waitress, and the hourly wage without tips was ridiculous. Please do not withhold a tip). The point is that because we do not have a real relationship with her, it is not that big of a deal to us. The wound from the unmet expectation, if there is one, is pretty superficial.

However, if our spouse rejects us through, let's say, an act of infidelity, it is much different. A promise was made, probably in front of friends, family, and God. There may be children involved now. This level of rejection can produce feelings of confusion, fear, hatred, and shame. For most, the longer we have been married, the more difficult it can be to overcome. Yet, a fairly new marriage infected by infidelity can be just as painful, if not more, when the offended partner already has unresolved issues related to betrayal.

This is similar to a child being rejected by a parent, the person who is expected to love and protect them at every turn. When this reasonable expectation or highly anticipated connection never materializes, it can produce wounding at a very deep level. The turbulent chaos created in a person's heart and mind can potentially cause such devastation it will bring the entire relationship to an abrupt end. Some people have even opted to cut all ties with parents who at one time turned their backs on them.

No one would fault the faithful husband for expecting fidelity from his disloyal wife or the innocent child for supposing their parent would love and protect them as a father or mother should. It is even understandable to expect good service from any business that aims to retain customers. All of these expectations are reasonable. We all go into situations with some sort of expectation.

The truth is, however, that some people can more easily bounce back from these broken expectations. They may even go through some of the levels of loneliness described earlier and come out stronger in the end. The intensity of the hurt and the individual's resolve will determine the outcome.

In that same line of thought, if you or someone you know tends to overreact to a simple snub in a public place from a perfect stranger, the intensity of the emotional backlash quite likely stems from an unresolved past rejection. In other words, a person who is highly sensitive and easily offended carries around a great deal of insecurity from past hurts, which in turn will create a greater intensity level of what they deem to be another rejection.

"For as he thinks in his heart, so is he."

PROVERBS 23:7 (NKJV)

Section 2

THE
TOXICITY OF
REJECTION

CHAPTER FIVE

IT CAN LEAD TO TRAUMA

"There are wounds that never show up on the body that are deeper and more hurtful than anything that bleeds."

LAURELL K. HAMILTON

Just days before I was born, my parents made the crazy decision to make the long drive from North Indiana to southwest Florida, the place I now call home. My mother was in her final month of pregnancy, but something in their young, wild hearts felt it was a clever idea to move closer to family before I was born. They packed everything up, piled it in the trunk of their car, and played Russian roulette with my birth as they made the decision to drive almost 1300 miles.

Before you form a disapproving opinion about what you may consider their recklessness, you need to know my parents were very young and living alone with no family around. To make matters worse, they were struggling financially. As with so many young couples, their naivety played a big part in their decision-making. I would guess that most of us have been there a time or two.

Mom was pretty uncomfortable on the trip, so they stopped quite often to help ease the discomfort of sitting in one position for so long. Any long journey in most vehicles can be challenging, so add the fact that you are a pregnant woman in your ninth month of pregnancy to the scenario, and the distress seems a bit more understandable. This made the situation a catch-22 because, of course, the regular stops only added to the length of their trip.

Two days into their drive, somewhere in northern Florida, the contractions set in. As you can imagine, there was a great deal of nervousness amongst these two noticeably young adults who were soon-to-be parents for the first time in their lives. My dad pulled into the closest hospital he could find as soon as he realized time was of the essence. It was in the beautiful town of Ocala that I made my grand entrance into the world.

Although it was meant to be a happy moment, the unexpected suddenness of labor pains, along with the overwhelming and unfamiliar hospital routine, made the day of my arrival a challenging experience for my mom. Tie that to the fact that she had no one, other than my dad, to offer her support or encouragement. This was new for him too, after all. Aside from my mother's dismal emotional state, everything else went well, given the circumstances.

About four or five days later, the hospital released us, and my parents were on the road again . . . this time with a tiny newborn in hand. They had less than five hours left to arrive at their destination, so again, with little money in their pocket, they made another crazy decision to finish the trip.

As my dad tells the story, Mom was doing her best to get comfortable as she tried to recuperate in the back seat of the car after just giving birth only a few days earlier. My persistent crying only added to her misery. Dealing with the physical anguish while trying to console a brand-new baby was a bit much for her. As her body tried to make sense of the distress that comes with childbirth, she entered the beginning stages of what is known today as the "baby blues." Understandably, it was more than my young nineteen-year-old mother could emotionally handle at the time.

STARTLING SMACKS

As luck would have it, or bad luck in my case, at the ripe age of around five days old, I received my first spanking in the back of a 1964 Buick. According to Dad, I had been crying quite a bit, and in Mom's inexperienced mind, she had run out of options, so as a last resort, she smacked my fat little thigh a couple of times hoping for some quiet. As you can probably guess, that did not happen. My crying only got worse. Chaos overtook the atmosphere in the car, and unfortunately, they were still a couple of hours away from their destination. Dad had no clue what to do. He decided to pull over, take me from my mom, and put me in the front seat with him for the rest of the ride. When we finally arrived, my aunts and Grandma were a breath of fresh air for them both.

I cannot say precisely what the effects of that sudden and unwarranted spanking did to me. Was it harsh enough to be considered traumatic? Quite possibly. My husband jokingly tells people that my reserved and suspicious persona was birthed at that very moment. I have wondered, from time to time, if that could be true.

Now, I obviously do not remember the spanking, but I am sure my tiny baby mind was shocked by the sudden and abrupt swat, most certainly creating confusion of some sort. After all, it came from the person I was most connected to, the one who carried me closest and, up until that moment, made me feel safe. It is possible, I would guess, that the event could have created a disruption in my first life connection.

I want to underscore that while my parents did believe in well-deserved spankings when we got older, this was not that. This dreadful moment was contrived from a combination and overload of everything my poor mother was going through during this very upsetting time of parenthood. It was as if a perfect storm of events made her emotionally glitch. I have been around long enough to know that under the right circumstances ("wrong" circumstances makes more sense), a person can become so overwhelmed with life and the issues it tends to bring, that they suddenly seem to snap.

Later in our childhood, spankings were rare since Mom preferred yelling. She was quite notoriously known in our neighborhood for her loud and distinct call. The area we lived in was modest in size, and everyone knew everyone. Mom would holler for us whenever she felt we had overstayed a visit while playing at a friend's home. In her mind, picking up the phone to call three or four different houses before finally locating us would take too long, so she would just yell out our names loudly from the top of her lungs. She knew someone would eventually hear her. The strategy was really quite effective.

INSTRUCTIONS ARE NOT ENOUGH

Let me just say I know firsthand that parenting is one of the most demanding jobs on the planet. When we leave the hospital with a newborn, most of us are supplied with a baby blanket, some formula, and a few diapers. I have continuously repeated the old cliché that no one gets an instruction manual on how to raise the brand-new human in our arms.

Ironically, though, while helping to organize things for my parents in their home a few years back, I came across a brochure that did just that. It was titled Infant Care and was published by the United States Department of Labor Children's Bureau. Since it was a 1934 copy, and I was born in 1970, I doubt Mom and Dad left that hospital in Ocala over fifty years ago with it in hand. One of their pastimes was collecting antiques, so my guess is the little booklet was part of their collection.

Nonetheless, there was a time when people used to get an instruction manual on raising a child. The introduction in this particular 1934 copy does essentially emphasize my point. The author explains it this way, "As soon as the baby is born, he begins to live in the surroundings that the parents have provided. Immediately, he begins to learn by his experiences. From the hour of birth, he learns from everything around him."

Halfway through the manual, the topic of punishment is addressed by noting it has no place in the first year of life and that slapping or punishment should never be resorted to with babies. There printed clear as day were the instructions on how a parent should never resort to physical mistreatment when dealing with a devastated baby or infant.

Although I have not birthed a child in almost three decades, I would bet that some type of literature or resource on caring for a newborn is sent home with today's new parents. Yet, I am woefully confident that there are still moms and dads who, despite a handbook and combined with all their good intentions, regrettably lose their cool trying to figure out how to quiet an inconsolable child. What that looks like for the everyday parent can range from yelling uncontrollably to giving an unexpected spanking. It is important to note that there are moms who are going through postpartum depression and find themselves acting grossly out of character due to a chaotic hormonal imbalance. No matter the reason or gravity, most overreacting parents are remorseful and experience bouts of shame after the fact.

The guilt, although not at the moment, derives from the parent's innate understanding that the child is helpless and needs them for security. For most, the lapse of control is rare and often short-lived. However, the problem lies in the belief that when a child experiences a disconnection through a loss of safety, there is no memory of it.

Nothing could be further from the truth, though. A child between the ages of 0–6 years old that experiences a frightening or violent event will have their sense of safety shattered, causing what is known as childhood trauma.

The gauntlet of experiences leading to childhood trauma are far and wide, and like adults, the individual effects range from person to person. While it is easy to recognize incidents such as the death of a parent, parental divorce, or physical and sexual abuse as traumatic, other experiences may be deemed less severe and have the same result.

THE MANY MYSTERIES OF REJECTION TRAUMA

This means that as innocent as it may be, a terrifying image, blaring sound, or a violent movement that is sudden and unexpected can have severe effects on an infant. Since the child is vulnerable and not emotionally developed, especially if their temperament is highly sensitive, they have no internal indication of how to begin to resolve the shock of what they have experienced. It is too much for their fairly new nervous system, and it may possibly register as a disconnection.

These disturbing events can interrupt vital parts of a child's development that happen before the age of three years old. The implications are that even if the hasty response comes from an act of overwhelming thoughtlessness and occurs just once or twice, it could cause problems for the child in the future. Some of these complications involve delayed language development, hindered social skills, poor emotional control, and impending connections with their parent and others.

My intent is not to applaud or defend reactions such as spanking or yelling, nor is it to discuss the anguish or possible dangers of postpartum depression. These are essential topics for another day. Instead, I want to highlight that a rejection endured at an early age can lead to trauma more often than we may realize or even wish to accept.

In our world, although some human involvement is the norm for almost every newborn child, the perfect love and security model most people believe should exist is not often the case. Experts claim this "perfect" model of security and love is necessary to create a solid foundation for a well-functioning human being.

THE MISUNDERSTANDINGS AROUND THE EFFECTS

Sadly, because we are built for this connection, the negative instances can signal danger and create mistrust and unhealthy defense mechanisms in a child who is in the foundational stages of their worldview. Although it is easy to conclude that the youngest of these children may have no memory of a parent's unexpected and hurtful reaction to their inconsolable cries, I would gather that the innocent child was, in some way, seen or unseen in that moment, negatively impacted by their adverse reaction. A short circuit in the essential connection occurred, per se.

Again, no matter our predisposition towards humanity, whether we are born with an extroverted or introverted personality, we all have a fundamental need to belong. Think of a crying newborn baby who is instantly calmed by the sound of his mother's voice. It was the voice he constantly heard while he grew and waited in her womb for nine months to enter the world. When mom lays him on her chest, he falls fast asleep because he recognizes that he is home, in a sense. If nothing else is wrong with the child, he is immediately comforted by the reconnection to his mother. Reassurance and peace are what every child needs. It is what every human being desires.

When we feel shocked, disconnected, or pushed away at any level, the effects of rejection feel unnatural and uncomfortable to us. Imagine what this does to an innocent child. Physical abuse, molestation, death, a car accident, or any shocking event will disrupt their intended perfect world. According to studies, children impacted by rejection are different socially and psychologically, showing signs of low self-esteem and self-adjustment, excessive dependency, and emotional instability. Their perception of the world is tainted by this sordid negativity.

The innocence of an infant or toddler will very likely feel the effects at a deeper level. The confusion alone would be enough to cause trauma. Ironically, the results are quite similar if the child witnesses something horrific, such as violent crime, parental abuse, or any cataclysmic event. Studies show these traumas become embedded in the brain. Whether it is a one-time hard, impactful occurrence or unintentional repeated incidents, you can rest assured there will be adverse effects to deal with in the future.

ADVERSE CHILDHOOD EXPERIENCES

Of course, if these instances are intentional with more severity or consistency for the child, the complications faced in adulthood are inevitable, as well as heightened. A study on these problems has grown popular within the last decade. The research looks at various aspects of life but focuses more on the relationship between the experiences of a child and their physical health in adulthood. You read that correctly. Amongst the many ways childhood trauma will negatively change your life, perhaps one of the most detrimental is your health.

Like me, you have heard that laughter is good medicine for the soul, and negative emotions, such as anger, are bad for your health. This study, known as Adverse Childhood Experiences, or ACE, shows that old cliches are more valid than we realize. Their findings show an obvious scientific connection between an extensive list of adversities in childhood, mental health issues, and physical diseases in adulthood. Experiences such as verbal, physical, and sexual abuse; emotional and physical neglect; being raised by a parent suffering through depression, mental illness, alcoholism, or drug addiction; watching a parent abuse the other parent; and losing home stability through a divorce, are all considered traumatic and possible causes of future problems. Recent studies added parental death, watching a brother or sister being abused, experiencing bullying from classmates or other adults, and growing up impoverished to the list of traumas.

These experiences are quite different from the ordinary childhood disturbances that come up in a child's life due to unforeseen circumstances or failures. There is a clear distinction in that these encounters are unpredictably frightening, prolonged, and stressful, and the child usually must fend for themselves due to the lack of support from the adults in their life.

They have found that the emotional shock and damage encountered as children changes the makeup of the brain and the condition of the immune system in negative ways. The research showed that traumatic events "trigger and sustain inflammation in both the body and brain, and they influence our overall physical health and longevity long into adulthood." Furthermore, the studies showed that the changes that occur direct how we will respond to our future surroundings, the people in our lives, and the relationships we build.

This does not mean all physical and mental ailments derive from a traumatic childhood. Common sense can tell us that there are things that we do, such as willingly putting toxic things into our bodies and minds, many times at excessive levels, which will affect our well-being. Of course, the question of whether these unhealthy choices stem from our disruptive childhood remains.

In other words, does compulsive eating, excessive alcohol drinking, smoking, or unwarranted drug consumption serve as a subconscious sedative for unresolved childhood rejection issues? If so, is this the explanation, or does it simply add to the rise of poor adult health in those who endured childhood trauma? Although I am not a scientist, these possible connections seem highly probable.

ACE is a fascinating study to consider if you can identify yourself or someone you love with these findings. The scientists who developed it created an assessment that takes the different adverse events we may have encountered as children and adolescents and then placed them into categories in the form of questions. They are based on the following experiences: physical, emotional, and sexual abuse; physical or emotional neglect; household dysfunctions occurring from mental illness; incarceration of a relative; substance abuse; witnessing the abuse of a parent or divorce.

The responses create an outcome that assigns a participant score ranging from 0 to 10, according to their "yes" responses. The higher the score, the more likely the participant will have future health issues. In other words, the more traumatic a person's childhood is, the higher the risks for potential problems. Nonetheless, the assessment could serve to put some questions to rest. (Appendix A)

"But whoever listens to me will dwell secure and will be at ease, without dread of disaster."

PROVERBS 1:33 (ESV)

CHAPTER SIX

ITS WEEDS WILL STRANGLE THE SEEDS

"'The kingdom of heaven may be compared to a man who sowed good seed in his field, but while his men were sleeping, his enemy came and sowed weeds among the wheat and went away.'"

JESUS, MATTHEW 13:24-25 (ESV)

S elf-awareness has become a huge buzzword in the world of self-improvement. It is demonstrated by an individual's capability to pay attention to oneself. This makes perfect sense in my line of business. If a person wants to focus on bettering themselves, taking a good, honest look at who they truly are inside is an excellent place to start. However, there is a lot more to it than just paying attention to ourselves.

Self-awareness has many different facets and levels to consider if someone genuinely wants to reach their full potential in life. Part of my work with clients who want to move from where they are to where they want to be is guiding them through this discovery process. Since the goal of these chapters is to focus on the ins and outs of rejection, and the topic of self-awareness would require its own book, we will keep it simple.

To keep from getting too deep into the weeds of psychology, we will stick to the two basic levels of external self-awareness: empathy and sympathy. Both are attributes that make up an individual's emotional intelligence. The two terms, empathy and sympathy, are similar and often confused, but they are not the same. The difference between the two can determine the outcome of a relationship.

SYMPATHY SHOULD LEAD TO EMPATHY

Empathy is the ability to see how you fit into the world and the lives of those around you. It is the recognition that others have feelings, too. The marvelous gift of empathy can provide the capacity to understand and, at times, even feel what others are going through. Empathy is the more advanced of the two, and the gift can be developed as a person matures.

On the other hand, sympathy begins to show itself earlier in a person's life, during the self-awareness phase. It entails a shared feeling of sadness, pity, or compassion for another person, and it is believed to be innate. As evidence, experts point to the crying response of a baby when they hear another baby in distress as if to signify that the sound of another suffering child troubles them. At about the one-year mark, there is a realization that the crying is not their own. Although they may not understand where the crying stems from, there could be an effort by the calm baby to comfort the other child through cooing or by attempting physical touch. Whatever means are utilized, there is evidence that they feel bad for the distraught child. This is sympathy in action.

In adulthood, sympathy may look like this: A coworker you just met misses work for a few days. You learn they had to go out of town to attend a family funeral. Your inclination would be to sympathize with them. This happens through an internal understanding that another person is suffering without really knowing them. You have compassion for them and feel sadness, but you may not necessarily feel what they are feeling. In an effort of consolation, you may verbally share your condolences or give them a sympathy card. You feel sorry for them because you understand that the loss of life is hard on people.

Empathy is the ability to place ourselves in someone else's shoes. It is possible if you recently lost a family member yourself and can personally relate to the loss. It is as if you are sensing the heartbreak from your memories all over again. If the coworker were a close friend, you would be more apt to empathize with them. However, seeing the pain through their eyes is different than just feeling bad for the other person. Empathy goes beyond sympathy and can sometimes signify a more mature emotional and mental state. A higher EQ, per se. The person willfully steps outside the circle of self, into a one-on-one connection.

Experts describe empathy as both a trait and a skill. While we all have the capability to empathize with others, normally, this does not happen by chance. Usually, it is modeled at home for a child. Children learn by simply watching an emotionally healthy mom or dad connect with the people in their lives. Of course, parents are not being heartless by any means when they do not take the time to teach the skill of empathy. Many are unaware of what constitutes empathy or that a child can be instructed explicitly in this area.

A SELF-CENTERED WORLD

If you look around, you can see the effects of this blind spot in the expansion of a self-centered generation. No offense to the youth of today. While I know many young adults who are pretty impressive in their nobility and generosity, it is hard to deny we are in an era drowning in what is known as narcissism. It is defined as an excessive preoccupation with oneself. The articles, podcasts, YouTube episodes, and books on the topic are endless. If you are familiar with the term, you probably have occasionally identified a few in your circles. A quick search on the Internet will lead you to the origin of this popular term.

Narcissus was a Greek mythological figure who was so attractive he fell in love with an image of himself he saw reflected in a pond of water. The myth carries different variations, but the central premise is based on the selfish way the character callously championed his ego, continuously believing he was above and better than everyone else.

In some extended sagas, Narcissus, who clearly lacks empathy, humiliates and rejects Echo, a nymph who is madly in love with him. In one version, she is completely consumed with attaining Narcissus' attention. Perhaps Echo believes if she succeeds, it will somehow reverse the pain of the rejection. In the end, Narcissus' cruelty and disregard for Echo devastate her to the point that she physically disappears, and all that is left in the end is her voice.

On a superficial level, this mythological story of rejection is the basis of the plot of countless Hollywood movies. You know, the film where the main character is emotionally crushed and tormented by the overtly egotistic antagonists in their life. Halfway through, they hit a metaphorical wall and realize they have lost all sense of who they truly are.

Encounters with individuals who live in their self-centered world are infinite. Not surprisingly, both men and women are caught up in these types of toxic relationships.

Considering all the rejection possibilities we have covered throughout these chapters, it is easy to see why so many people are walking around broken inside, struggling to relate to others. The sharp edges of their shattered soul have carelessly cut those who got too close. In many cases, we were the ones who bled for them. It is that pain that explains the pull to such storylines. Sales tend to be high in a film with a "good versus evil" scenario that ends with the narcissistic villain being put in their place.

I can attest to my own fondness for this theme since I have had my connections with narcissists. Had I been smarter about where I was emotionally, had more knowledge about the intentions of those I was drawn to, or been more discerning, I may have avoided some of the pain I endured in my youth. I must confess, part of my inclination towards watching women on the screen come to their senses and defeat their destructive desires while the villain gets what is coming to him sits very well with me. I find this entertainment a sort of loose redemption for my past heartaches.

NARCISSUS ROAMS THE HALLS IN HIGH SCHOOL

On a more serious level, perhaps, is the way this mythological story parallels much of what happens in the school hallways of today's pre-teens and teens. From my time in the classroom, I can tell you the "mean girl" and "bullying" situations you hear about are very real, and they happen more often than I would like to admit.

The upsurge in this insensitive age has prompted many school districts to prioritize social-emotional learning in their curriculum. In an effort to defeat the self-centeredness of today and build up the child's emotional well-being, SEL (Social Emotional Learning) programs are designed to teach the skills required to develop self-responsibility and accountability, as well as the empathy needed to treat others humanely. However, because this training is in its infancy stages, many who graduated before the onset of this new movement are still walking around clueless.

This is where the problem lies for those who lack empathy and have yet to realize the world does not revolve around them. The external or "other-awareness" either has not fully developed or has been disrupted. There are a variety of reasons why this happens.

Interruptions occur when those who have been raised to appreciate and love others from an early age encounter heartbreaking or toxic relationships. It is possible to have been raised in a good moral home where good ethics, sympathy, and empathy were modeled and taught, and the individual shockingly squanders their character due to the powerful effects of rejection.

In other words, despite having a decent upbringing, some become someone their parents barely recognize. The deep sting of rejection outside the home can take a once compassionate individual and turn them into a heartless young lady or young man. It is as if they have suffered an identity crisis at an early age.

A FRAGILE MOMENT IN TIME

Years ago, as a middle school educator, I had the privilege of heading up an afterschool club for young ladies between the ages of eleven and fourteen. The name of the group was G.I.R.L. It was an acronym that stood for Girls Inspiring Real Living. We met every Tuesday for an hour and a half with the sole purpose of equipping the participants to deal with the everyday issues and pressures of growing up. Each meeting had a different theme and activity built around biblical concepts, always aiming to encourage and support the young ladies. The objective was to create a rapport based on trust and respect in an effort to encourage the transparency necessary for them to comfortably share and discuss everyday insecurities. As a confidant for the girls, I was privy to confidential conversations where they openly discussed their mental battles and relationship struggles.

If you have forgotten what it was like to be a girl in her early teens or are of the opposite sex, you must know that this is an extremely tough time for them. These young ladies are desperately trying to fit in, all while their bodies are changing and their hormones are raging. The plethora of emotions they face as they struggle to make sense of who they are and where they fit in, along with trying to figure out their feelings, puts them on a rollercoaster of confusion, riding them straight for the claws of rejection. Some grown women will attest that this time in a girl's life can be traumatic.

The girls that joined G.I.R.L. were all different in many ways. The group had an array of personalities and perspectives, but one thing connected them all. Their parents sent them to school believing their daughters would uphold their family values and maintain their self-dignity. I cannot tell you whether these parents forgot their preteen years or did not understand how times change with each generation, but many believed their child was ready to independently take on the world, at least Monday through Friday. Through the eyes of an educator and my own experience, I can assure you that allowing these young girls to fend for themselves at such a delicate age was, and continues to be, a big mistake.

Please do not misunderstand me. I am not advocating for unending dependency or raising babies who grow up to be thin-skinned adults offended at every turn because mom and dad never allowed them to fight their own battles. I am simply raising a red flag for parents who want to give independence too abruptly, too soon, or without acknowledging what their sweet child will encounter in most middle school hallways.

When they enter this new world, many girls face social fears and are psychologically vulnerable at levels they have not known before. They go through these uncertainties all on their own. Rejection is a huge fear, but as noted in the first section, it is an unavoidable reality. Teasing, bullying, gossiping, being excluded, or being ganged up on certainly do happen, making surviving socially a top priority for this age group. The drive to be liked, to fit in, and to be perfect for some leads them to conform to a person their parents never expected.

My own parents were relatively involved in my elementary school days. Yet, for whatever reason, they felt I could handle myself in middle school, so they mistakenly let go of the reigns way too soon. In my days of holding teacher conferences, I can testify to this same line of thinking in the many parents I met. When I had the opportunity to speak to them, one of my pleas was for them to continue to be involved in their child's education.

The memories I have from my preteen years are miserable. In fact, the grown-up me is pretty disappointed with a lot of the choices of my youth. All the success I had earned in my elementary years came to a screeching halt when I entered middle school. My grades took a dive, and my parents' expectations were drowned out by foolish behaviors meant to hide my insecurities. I will say in those days and the years that followed, my peaking interest in boys, paired with my need to be accepted, only served to heighten the mortification and betrayal of the real me.

This is one of the main reasons why, on more than one occasion, I invited parents whose child was starting to test the waters of rebellion to come and sit in throughout their school day. Of course, it rarely happened. Sadly, the student in question usually talked mom or dad out of doing something they deemed outrageous. In their mind, it would destroy them socially.

This is where most parents who intended to stay involved gave up. The child, who once begged them to have lunch with them in second grade, now seemed embarrassed by their presence among their peers. Ironically, Mom and Dad experienced the sting of rejection, too.

BELIEF SYSTEMS BROKEN

During my initial years as a middle school educator, social media was nearly nonexistent, so the young ladies got their likes from the girls' approval in their sphere and the popular boys in their grade. As you might imagine, that drive for approval caused a lot of drama in their social circles. For whatever reason, the yearning to be accepted was so intense with some, that it led them to throw out all the morals and standards their parents had worked so hard to instill in them.

One gal in our G.I.R.L. group shared the torment she endured at the hands of a resentful classmate. Evidently, this fellow student was quite bothered by the idea that her twelve-year-old boyfriend was paying too much attention to this girl. It turned out the envious young lady became so enraged she physically assaulted her during their lunch period in front of their peers. To make matters worse, the boyfriend decided his flirtation was not worth the trouble and sought cowardly redemption for his roving eyes. He put on a little show to get back into the good graces of his bitter girlfriend. Intending to cause further humiliation, he verbally ridiculed the young lady in front of his buddies.

Watching as she uncontrollably sobbed and told her story to the group was heart-wrenching for me.

Parents, this will be the toughest part to listen to. For some of you moms, it may stir up some traumatic emotions from your own youth. This beautiful young lady was not crying because she was embarrassed or because she did not do more to defend herself. Instead, through tear-filled eyes, the only thing that concerned her was figuring out how to get these two cruel individuals back on her good side.

All the values her parents had instilled in her meant nothing at that moment. The talks about having the courage to stand up for what she believes, being resilient in the face of challenges, and always maintaining her self-respect all went out the window. Her only focus was on how she was perceived by the same people who had recently shamed her. She desperately wanted to be accepted back into the group.

Again, if we are unfamiliar with everything that comes with this period in a young girl's life, and I am sure it is not much better for the boys, our instinct may be to dismiss it with a slight cringe, believing they will get over it eventually. Yet research shows that when an adult is snubbed publicly, there is a flood of emotions and mental distress that can even affect the quality of their sleep. If this happens to most grown people, it is hard to imagine what it does to an innocent child who has yet to develop the skills needed to cope with the flood of emotions that come from rejection.

From a child's perspective, social rejection, especially repeated social rejection, can create such intense fear and self-doubt it will choke out the good seeds planted by the parent and alter their persona. If left untended, you can expect to see the fruit of negativity in their later years.

UNATTENDED WEEDS SMOTHER YOUR JOY

As part of the women's ministry in my home church, I have had the privilege of meeting many beautiful ladies from all walks of life. And across all backgrounds, there were always those who came with a pressing issue from their past. Some had naively entered into toxic relationships; others were heartbroken by a thoughtless spouse or rebellious child. The most harrowing stories to hear were of the ones who had been abused or rejected as a child and could not shake free.

Not to minimize the hurt of anyone, but there was a distinct difference in those who carried pain from their youth. Maybe it was because they had held it for so long or because it happened at such a vulnerable stage in their life. Whatever the reason, they almost seemed to wear what the Bible refers to as a crushed spirit.

The harm done to the human ego by a cruel encounter, especially at such a tender age, can cause a negative shift in the perspective of the person affected. Value systems are overridden, and a person's entire personality can go from trusting to cynical in some instances.

SOCIAL MEDIA SUFFOCATES SELF-CONFIDENCE SEEDS

Another heartbreaking experience that can cause an interruption in a person's belief system comes from the influence of the media. Although I know many adults affected by this platform, it is especially prevalent in the younger generation. For the past couple of decades, the change in how people connect is clear to everyone on the planet. These once-nonexistent social networks have provided a great deal of the desired connection, even if the connection is superficial. Since many children and adults alike have a fear of missing out, the number of users on platforms such as Snapchat, Instagram, Facebook, and TikTok, to name a few, has grown exponentially.

If you or your child spend extensive amounts of time on social media, you must understand what you are up against. The fact that misuse of this tool causes the human connection to decrease, sleep to be interrupted, and attention spans to shorten should be enough to sound the alarm. However, what it does to the reality of who we truly are can devastate the self-esteem of a once confident individual.

What we see online may have some realistic undertones, and many innocently enough just want to share their victories and milestones. But the truth is people posting sometimes brush up their pictures and pump up their stories. You will rarely find someone sharing their garbage with the world.

Before you know it, you are subconsciously comparing yourself to what you see, no matter how unreal it may be. You begin to focus on what you do not have, ironically rejecting yourself. The effects that come from losing likes or followers simply serve to multiply those negative emotions. The more time you spend browsing, the greater the risks are for anxiety and depression. The countless cases where people develop eating disorders, self-loathing opinions, suicidal ideation, or worse, are astronomical. And it is all due to living their life through a screen that pushes out a lot of fictional and misleading information.

Like with most things, there are positive factors that come from social media. However, if you are struggling to break free of past rejections, it is probably a good idea to limit your time on these platforms or shut them down altogether. Perhaps you believe this does not apply to you. I do know some people want nothing to do with this type of interaction. If you are one of them, I applaud you since (by design) the pull of social media is considered more addictive than smoking cigarettes.

However, if you are part of these platforms, which most of us are, I want to present a one-question quiz: a warning test of sorts. Can you remember the last time you went an entire twenty-four hours without checking your phone or other devices of your choice? While a whole day may be an extreme measure in our world of technology, how about twelve hours, half a day?

If the answer is no, you may want to reevaluate your stance. These platforms, initially meant for entertainment, could be shaping your thoughts, ideas, and even your perception in a negative way. It could be the culprit for unexpected feelings of sadness, anxiety, and a variety of other toxic emotions. Without realizing it, a rejection of oneself has opened the door to mental distress.

> *"But while everyone was sleeping, his enemy came and sowed weeds among the wheat, and went away."*
>
> MATTHEW 13:25

CHAPTER SEVEN

IT WILL POISON A TENDER SOUL

"If you live for people's acceptance, you will die from their rejection."

LECRAE

M om and Dad were fifteen and sixteen when they decided to run away together. That sounds young, but it was normal in the 1960s Hispanic culture. Add that to the environment they lived in, and it makes their actions even less shocking. Both of my parents grew up in what would be considered less-than-healthy functioning homes. Their surroundings played a significant role in their eloping, perhaps in an attempt to find solace and comfort elsewhere.

THE TRAIL OF PHYSICAL AND VERBAL ABUSE

My father was trying to escape a controlling and abusive home life. He suffered a great deal of verbal and physical cruelty at my grandfather's hands. My dad's brothers and sisters told of the anger, intimidation, and pure trepidation they endured growing up. My grandma, his wife, had a huge heart but was quite timid and an extremely passive lady, thus suffering abuse at his hands herself. Although she loved her children, she rarely, if ever, mustered up the courage to stand up to her husband's cruelty towards them. My poor dad and his siblings were left to fend for their selves, so you can understand why he was strongly inclined to leave his unstable home at such an early age.

Later in life, it was evident to me, at least, that my grandfather's verbal and physical rage brought many destructive effects into the lives of my aunts and uncles. Three of them lost their lives in alcohol-related accidents, and three died of liver cirrhosis. Eleven of the fourteen divorced. Today, two daughters and a son (my dad) remain. I got to know all but two of my aunts and uncles on my dad's side of the family fairly well. Despite growing up in a swamp of toxicity, they were genuinely kindhearted. Yet, while they all were seemingly good people, I look back now and can see how my grandfather's abusive words and actions crippled their self-worth.

THE SIGNIFICANCE OF FATHERS

Physical and verbal abuse at the hands of the person meant to protect you is a form of rejection at the highest level. As much as today's culture would like to deny the importance of a father's role in a child's life, he is indeed a significant player. His actions and presence, or lack thereof, will aid in shaping the child into a future adult. An "unabusive" yet detached father can have similarly devastating results in a child's life.

This means a dad can be present physically but show little to no emotional concern for a child, and the outcome is relatively similar to that of a child raised in a fatherless home. A present father who shows affection and support will undoubtedly help in the healthy emotional development of his child. Studies show a direct correlation between children with absent fathers and teen violence, suicide attempts, drop-out rates, and drug use.

On the flip side, children with toxic fathers in the home can go to extremes in adulthood, subconsciously trying to prove their worth through high accolades in an effort to silence the abusive and demeaning voices in their heads. This is harder to spot. Most people would not suspect a high-achieving perfectionist of having issues of self-worth. The person with an abusive childhood would have to come to terms with the lack of peace in their soul and take an honest look at what truly drives their desire to succeed.

Fathers are meant to be a covering of protection against any wrongdoing to the child, scripturally speaking. He is the one meant to lead the child and give them their sense of identity by demonstrating the heavenly Father's nature. When this is nonexistent, individuals tend to have many relationship issues. Women are inclined to have low self-esteem, and their choice of partners and a high tolerance for abuse will reflect as such. Men will often mimic their father's abusive treatment of their mother towards their partner, children, employees, or coworkers, and they are more apt to be involved in destructive behaviors. Both sexes will be prone to drug abuse, alcoholism, domestic violence, and other damaging behaviors.

ABANDONMENT LEADS TO FEAR AND OTHER MYSTERIOUS BEHAVIORS

My mom's childhood, although void of physical abuse, had its share of hardships. She told us about the abandonment by her birth father at three months of age.

Abandonment, a powerful form of rejection, points to someone in our life leaving and not returning. When a critical part of the child's life is absent, you better believe it will generate inadequate thoughts in their mind. When the mother, who is called to comfort and nurture, or the father, whose duty is to protect and love, willingly forsake their responsibility to the child, fear will undoubtedly set in to taint the child's future. These children are subconsciously left wondering what they did wrong. They develop trust issues and feelings of inadequacy. The fear that will rear its head is due to the possibility of future abandonment, which can be seen in a person's life in several ways.

Now understand, this is not intended to be a diagnosis but simply a confirmation of specific indicators that may be causing you a lack of peace. These markers also fall into vastly different forms on the emotional spectrum. As I stated earlier, people who seem to have it all together can suffer from rejection, and you would never know from what you see on the outside. Some of the most common signs are low self-esteem, constant battles with anxiety or depression, an outwardly hardcore or tough exterior, intentional separation from others, and an unhealthy tolerance of poor treatment from others to ensure they are not left again.

Additionally, you can find them involved in relationships with individuals incapable of providing emotional or physical security. This form of self-sabotage, either due to a sense of unworthiness or to build a wall against future commitment, has led many into the arms of toxic people. They waste a great deal of time trying to "fix" and figure out the relationship. They wonder why their partner lies, cheats, disrespects, or disappears on them consistently. Even through the constant chaos, there is a subconscious belief that future abandonment can somehow be evaded.

On the other end of the scale, a very well-put-together individual can tend to be a huge critic of others or themselves. In the frame of high self-esteem, the person can be an extremely high achiever. Everything they do and say is usually premeasured. No mistakes are allowed, deterring any possibility of criticism through an appearance of perfection. This is much different than doing things with a mindset of excellence.

This person may hold a very unrealistic bar for those in their circle, making others cringe in their presence and run in the other direction. Ironically, they are creating a stimulus for more rejection. Their perfectionism leads them to often set unreachable goals for themselves, too, causing them to fail to attain the goal or procrastinate; both will cause them to beat themselves up mentally for not doing better. While these individuals can suffer from eating disorders, depression, and anxiety, the correlation between suicide and perfectionism is astounding. Almost sixty percent of families related to those who took their own life describe the person as a perfectionist.

ABANDONMENT IS NOT ALWAYS CUT AND DRY

Again, any of these behaviors can signal rejection injuries to a tender soul who missed out on the love, care, and protection every child is entitled to. Some of these behaviors can point to other anomalies in the human soul of an adult, such as immaturity or naïveté. However, if they are paired with an uneasiness in the person's spirit that causes them to feel as if no one is really there for them, and they can link it with some type of parental issue, abandonment is likely the culprit.

It is essential to repeat that the consequences of abandonment can occur in the heart of a child with a parent present physically but missing emotionally. Perhaps this is the most difficult of all the wounds of rejection to identify. If a child is physically abused, there are outward signs. You may see unexplainable bruises, cuts, or breaks. If a child is neglected, there are also outward signs. The child may be dirty, hungry, and sleepy from staying up all night without supervision. If the child is missing a parent or both parents from their life, someone could quickly point to the absence as a reason for the circumstances of the abuse or neglect.

However, it is not as evident if both parents are in the picture and present themselves as fairly attentive in the public eye, but a lack of love, attention, or nurturing occurs behind closed doors. What makes it more difficult for some who have experienced this type of childhood is that they innocently believed this was the norm. I mean, as children, what could we really compare it to since the material things of life were readily available? A distant father or mother who provides food, clothes, medicine, and shelter delivers all the necessary tools for physical survival.

Emotional abandonment leaves out the less obvious: attention, affection, and approval. While these are all needed to cultivate healthy emotional growth in a child, their omission is not so noticeable to the seeing eye, and many of us never realize it could be the underlying predicament of our own issues.

The problem arises when we are in adulthood experiencing a numbness or emptiness in our soul, and we cannot understand why.

You cannot point to a childhood issue causing the feeling of desolation, fear, insecurity, or other puzzling emotions you are experiencing. Perhaps your parent was missing because they worked long hours to provide the best for you, traveled a lot due to their work, or were stationed across the globe regularly due to their military responsibilities. They did their best to connect with you. Understand this: the reason a parent is emotionally absent matters not. When that connection is missing or broken, it could affect you negatively, even after many years.

An indicator of abandonment issues is found in the connections people are involved in. People who have faced abandonment in childhood tend to fall on two far ends of the relationship spectrum, all in an effort to avoid further pain.

There are those who will have a challenging time allowing others to get close to them. These individuals will either refrain from forming connections or deliberately sabotage them, for fear of facing rejection again. On the other side of the coin, there will be those who seem to either feel unworthy or have difficulty being alone and will lower their expectations for a partner in their life. Ironically, the significant other often adds to their insecurities through mistreatment such as control, verbal or physical abuse, and withholding love and affection. Instead of moving towards healing, they reinforce the misplaced beliefs they gathered amid their childhood rejection.

ABANDONMENT PRODUCES FEAR AND OTHER CONFUSING BEHAVIORS

Thankfully, there was a bit of buffering in Mom's abandonment story. Ama Maria, my mother's mom, was able to withstand some of the baby's father's abandonment consequences with her parents' help. My grandma and my mother lived with my great-grandparents, and they loved Mom like their own. The two stayed there until the man I came to know as my grandfather entered the picture. He was a kind, hardworking soul who absolutely doted on my grandmother. They married shortly after, and as the family grew, Mom gained a heap of siblings.

Compared to my dad, life was much calmer in Mom's home but far from perfect. She loved her brothers and sisters, and they loved her back. However, as the only child to a different father, Mom always had the lingering feeling of being the family outsider. She would tell us about her sibling squabbles and how there were times in the heat of the moment when one of her sisters would remind her that she was not truly one of them. Of course, they were kids and did not know any better. Yet, that did not eliminate the sting of their words. It could have been the rejection of her birth father or perhaps the occasional moments of snubbing from my aunts. Still, she held a tight sense of rejection, shouldering a feeling that her stepdad, my grandfather, never saw her as his own daughter either.

My parents experienced childhood rejection through neglect, abandonment, and emotional, verbal, and physical abuse. Sadly, the rejection was more profound because it came at the hands of those who were supposed to love them the most. Both were the oldest in their line of siblings. Mom was one of nine children, and Dad, after the passing of his older brother, was one of thirteen brothers and sisters. Each was the eldest child, so one could say it offered them an open invitation to being in charge, consequently feeding the dominant personality they were both born with. You can understand how their position and responsibilities in their home shaped their way of thinking. If you add that to the conditions they were brought up in, you may very well imagine the chaos that dimmed their relationship when they decided to run away and make a life together.

Let's just say two very strong-willed parents raised me. Mom and Dad, both very young and each with an inclination towards being in control, made for quite a hectic childhood. Their unrestrained arguments, at times, turned physical, and their baggage of rejection added to an already emotional rawness. At some level, it limited their capacity to express their love fully. Like all of us, they did not know what they did not know.

Now, please do not misinterpret what I am saying. Mom and Dad were big-hearted people who did their best with what they knew. We were always clean, healthy, and fed. They expected us to be respectful and well-behaved around family and friends, and we were required to do our very best in school. Always.

Discipline and love, spattered with hints of encouragement and affection, were a regular part of our childhood. I use the word "spattered" intentionally. Mom and Dad were strict, so we spent much of our time under watchful eyes. But the rockiness of their relationship took a front seat in our lives and, for the most part, blinded them to the typical emotional needs of a child. That is not to say that we did not receive encouragement, affection, and all the other beautiful gifts a parent provides. It just happened to be hindered and inconsistent since attention to it was eaten up by constant fighting and bickering.

The pain of the damage they carried from their childhood was never recognized or healed, for that matter. The effects came out in many different ways for both of them, typically ending in some kind of physical altercation. God had created two tender souls, but their childhood surroundings emotionally wrecked them. Although they were unaware, their love for each other was never fully expressed. It was constantly interrupted by the thoughts, beliefs, ideas, actions, and reactions produced inside their soul before they ever even met. Like most people, they had accepted the constant state of turmoil they had always known as the norm for their marriage.

We were much more connected to our mother. She was a nurturer by nature, and for all intents and purposes, while life was far from perfect, she did experience love and witnessed it growing up amidst the rejection. Dad got the shorter end of the stick. Naturally, it was harder to connect with him since he grew up in a home where connection rarely if ever, happened. Instead, it was replaced by belittling and beatings from our grandfather. I believe that because he never truly experienced the love every child deserves, especially from a father, it ruined his ability to fully appreciate my mother's deep love for him in their younger years. His brokenness blinded him to the blessings in his life as well. Unfortunately, that same distorted ability created somewhat of a gap between him and his own children.

THE POISON IS ALMOST ALWAYS PASSED ON

Millions of families across the globe begin their lives this way. While they may be aware of the basics of parenting, they do not know the reality of their brokenness. This is not at all finger-pointing; this is an admission of my own shortcomings and the experience of many people I have had the privilege of counseling. I have seen it time and again. People commit to a relationship with another human, pushing down all the hurts they have gathered along the way. As they try to move forward with their lives without an actual handbook on how to do this thing called adulthood, they move forward with the examples seen in their own families, as fragmented as they were. As my parents did, most will just do their best with what they know.

Let me reassure you there are millions of people who have suffered tremendously at the hands of their parents. I do not want to minimize that at all. I have heard stories that are so heartbreaking they seem unreal. What I describe to you is insignificant compared to what many of you have faced. My point is that the residue of brokenness often transfers over into the lives of those we love.

Quite frankly, we were not overlooked deliberately or even noticeably. Our family photos with two smiling parents surrounded by four well-groomed, sharply dressed, and rather attractive children are proof. Emotionally, however, it was a different story for me.

As a little girl, I had no idea what was happening in my soul. There was no awareness of what witnessing constant hostility between two people, who, in between the fighting, professed their love for one another, was doing to my emotions. There was no awareness of what watching my mother fly into a reasonable rage because she had caught wind of another one of my father's infidelities was doing to my mind. There was no awareness of what the internal desire to connect, obstructed constant clashes, was doing in my will. The unseen battle was continuous, and so, like many of us, I just soldiered on.

Even later in life, as I seemingly made bad decision after bad decision, I still had no understanding as to why I veered towards making outlandishly harmful choices. Like most of us, this was my life, and I did my best to live each day despite the fruit of my decisions. Then, I unknowingly carried my childhood toxicity into two marriages.

Ironically, the men I was drawn to also brought in their own rejection issues. The first marriage was short-lived and aggravated my soul issues by pouring salt in the wounds and intensifying all the negative outlooks and emotions I had been collecting. The failure of it all grew the bitterness and insecurities I had carried around for years.

Since I was completely unaware of the status of my heart and healing was not even in my vocabulary, I abruptly flew into my second marriage after my divorce. Trust me, when I say abruptly, it is not an understatement. One of the many pieces of evidence of being wounded is the incapacity of being alone. I remember my aunt gently warning me about what she deemed a rather careless decision. She said, "You need to be wise. The last thing you want to do is jump from the frying pan into the fire."

She was right, of course. I took the leap; the fire was hot, and I absolutely suffered many burns. My method for doing life in those days was letting the way the wind blew lead me to my choices instead of thinking things through. The hidden brokenness I carried around gave me a sense of unworthiness. I assume some people could not tell by looking at me, but because I believed I did not deserve any better, I quickly latched on to anything that gave me the slightest feeling of worth.

Coincidently, my second and current marriage started similarly to the first. Looking back, it is clear that both my husband and I lacked any sense of inner peace. While there were never any physical altercations, the atmosphere in our home mimicked the one I grew up in.

My husband was raised and adopted by his grandparents. His mother had him at the tender age of fourteen. Burdened by the weight of adolescence, she recognized she was not prepared to care for him. His father was also absent from the picture. David was the pride and joy of his grandparents. They loved him unconditionally, and they ensured he lacked nothing in life. As far as David was concerned, his grandfather Joe, who brought him comfort and guidance, was his dad. However, there was no denying the rejection he carried around in his soul. The weight of it cast a shadow on our marriage, threatening the very foundation of our relationship in the earlier years. The impact was so profound that divorce was seriously contemplated at one point. That story is for another book.

We, however, are part of the fortunate ones. God, in all His grace and mercy, has done a great work in healing David's heart. And breathed new life and restored our marriage. Thirty years later, we are still reaping the blessings from surrendering to the transformative power of His divine love.

No matter what anyone tells you or how wonderful the circumstances may seem, there is often, if not always, a battle in the mind of a child who believes they have been abandoned or rejected in some way by a parent or parents. Their guardians or adoptive parents can love them with all that is within them and provide a secure life, yet the question of why they were not wanted by their biological parents always lingers beneath the surface. They may not be completely aware of it, but it is a reality that comes with many wounds and scars.

Of course, the extent of the pain will vary from person to person. But if it is never addressed, more often than not, the person will carry the hurt into their future relationships, cutting and tainting the people they love.

WE DON'T KNOW WHAT WE DON'T KNOW

It is the same story for almost all of us who have innocently lived through some form of rejection during our years of upbringing. There is a pattern set inside of us, and we are bound to recreate it in some form later in life. It stains us from within. We mistakenly think we have pushed past it, convincing ourselves that this is just how it has to be, and then unknowingly carry the effects of the poison into every area of our future life.

We grow up completely unaware of God's best for us. Along the way, there are indicators and subtle signs that point to those plans. There is a strong desire to be loved and comforted, but when those things do not come to fruition, we just go with it. After all, you cannot miss something you have never had before.

For those of us who may have neglect and abuse thrown into the mix, we create self-defense mechanisms and never even truly realize it is happening. Our soul begins to generate ways to cope as we learn to live without the things God intended for us.

In the remake of the movie Father of the Bride, Steve Martin plays George Banks in a film that gives a picture of a perfect family. George, a doting dad who is not ready for his little girl to be married, is a bit grumpy, old-fashioned, and overprotective of his daughter, Annie.

This is one of my favorites, an all-time classic movie. It is hilarious and heartwarming, but I remember watching it for the first time and thinking how foreign the relationship between George and Annie was for me. While I understand Hollywood has a way of exaggerating life, I know some children, indeed, have been blessed by this bond with their parents.

Although the relationship between Annie and George was very moving, I suddenly realized at the age of eleven years that my life was missing that connection. While I can attest to a childhood with a grumpy, old-fashioned, and overprotective father, I have to say I was denied the relationship part as a young girl. Not intentionally, of course. I understand that wholeheartedly now, so no blame falls on my dad. The only example he had of how a man treats his children came from the cruelty of my grandfather. The abuse he grew up in created a disconnection he was not even aware of. Like many fathers, my father did not know what he did not know.

The truth is we live in a world where a father is sometimes missing entirely, and the implications that come with his absence are heartbreaking. There is no doubt that when a child, boy or girl, has a strong, healthy bond with their father or father figure, the positive impact in their life is undeniable. There truly is no substitute for a real father.

The Father of the Bride portrays a connection that does and can, in fact, exist between daughters (sons, too) and dads. Yet, our current culture proves that many cannot relate to the characters in the movie. Perhaps you or someone you know was spared from the toxicity, and you can relate. If so, consider yourself one of the blessed ones. In a world that so desperately needs healing, be sure to pass it on.

"When my father and mother have forsaken me, the Lord will take me up."

PSALM 27:10

CHAPTER EIGHT

IT BREEDS DYSFUNCTION AND DISEASE

*"Family is supposed to be our safe haven. Very often
it is where we find the deepest heartache."*

IYANLA VANZANT

My parents were together for almost sixty years. They gave us a comfortable home, hearty meals, clean clothes, and protected us to the best of their ability. They raised four respectful children with successful lives of their own. However, if you allowed the experts to delve a little deeper and asked them for an analysis of my childhood family, they would quickly identify us as dysfunctional.

While this may sound like an ungrateful description of the wonderful people who provided everything we needed while growing up, hear me out before you stone me. Studies show that over seventy percent, and probably closer to eighty percent, of families fall into the same category. This high number indicates that most people unknowingly come from dysfunctional homes. The fact that you are reading this book tells me that you or someone you know is probably part of this high statistic.

People are flawed; you should remind yourself that the *Leave It to Beaver* portrayal of the picture-perfect home and the *Brady Bunch* textbook blended family on television were all fictional characters.

Please understand I am not suggesting dysfunction in a family should be acceptable, but the numbers do sadly support that it seems to be the norm. This explains the numerous divorces, social altercations, and mental health issues, like depression and anxiety, plaguing our world today. It also points to the fact that seven out of the ten reading these pages likely grew up in a home the experts would describe as such. Dysfunctional describes more of us than we would probably like to admit.

THE DISGUISE OF THE DYSFUNCTIONAL FAMILY

If you recall the ACE study at the beginning of this section, it provided a risk assessment created for the study with ten questions. The first half deals with personal issues such as stressful situations endured as a child or an adolescent. The latter half refers to situations with other members of our family. The entirety of the list focuses on family dysfunction.

To put things into perspective, let us examine the other supposedly twenty to thirty percent of the population: the functional family. A functional upbringing can be described as a family that works. In their homes, children are taught how to behave and think responsibly, to self-regulate positive and negative feelings, and to connect with people in a healthy way. People brought up in these ways are not perfect either. Still, they do have the skills necessary to become effective adults who live healthy emotional lives and contribute positively to the world around them without the excess baggage. Because rejection is uncommon or highly limited in these households, they produce children who can communicate, care, and commit healthily.

As adults, they are mindful of what a good relationship should look like and are resilient enough to bounce back from a disrespectful dismissal in their later years. When they are rejected, you will probably find they are wise and brazen enough to turn around and confidently walk away instead of staying and brooding. Most of these individuals living in a high-functioning home could spot the toxicity a mile away. They often will steer clear of the turmoil emitted by these emotionally wounded people.

In The Dictionary of Modern Medicine, the term dysfunctional is defined as a family with multiple internal conflicts, such as sibling rivalries, parent-child conflicts, domestic violence, mental illness, single parenthood, or external conflicts, such as alcohol or drug abuse, extramarital affairs, gambling, unemployment, or any influences that affect the basic needs of the family.

Perhaps some of the things listed make you cringe because they are all too familiar. Considering the high statistics identifying this particular group, many could raise their hand to qualify. Please do not fret. You are in good company; it includes me. While I cannot check off all of these boxes, there are enough on the list that impacted me in such a way that some basic needs of the human soul could not be met.

Throughout many years spent teaching, counseling, and coaching, I have had the privilege of holding profound conversations about insecurity with people from all walks of life, individuals who seemingly have everything in life going for them, and people at the top of their game in their careers and professions. These are people that you and I look up to and admire. They look and act the part. They are everything we want to be when we grow up. Yet if you get close enough, you can see the hurt.

At first, I was stunned that they, too, amid their success, battled with self-doubt. These seemingly larger-than-life individuals struggled with the pesky voice of uncertainty we all hear in our heads, too. There was a similarity shared by many of them. A large portion of these people admittedly were raised in a home that would clearly fit the definition of dysfunctional. In my conversations with them, they too desperately wanted to make sense of past rejections. They appeared to be on a mission to somehow avoid another haunting reencounter of an earlier rebuke.

One gentleman, in particular, stands out in my mind. I met him at a business building conference a few years back, where we participated in an activity asking the group members to identify the purpose of our own business.

We were given different colored index cards and asked to write out the identifying goal to signal that our business was finally a success. For example, "My business will be successful when annual profits exceed two hundred thousand dollars." That was the easy part. Next, we had to identify and write out three to four conflicting thoughts that kept us from reaching the goal we were aiming for, then share them with our group partner. Easy to write, maybe, but not so easy to admit out loud, especially in front of complete strangers.

This gentleman, who happened to be the president of a prestigious committee in his organization and was quite successful in his community of peers, went first. As he started to share his roadblocks, he visibly began to cry when the subject of his childhood came up. His conflicting thoughts came from the voice and words of a verbally abusive mother. As a little boy, she constantly told him that he was worthless, always with a tirade of profanities to accompany the insults. He was a grown man, savoring the bounties of a successful life as far as the eye could see. But internally, he was being tormented in his soul by the poisonous words of a mother who no longer even had a say in how he lived his life. His sobs became more intense as he described his mother's present suffering in the latter stages of dementia.

He now understood and had accepted the fact the woman he knew as his mom had lived most of her life battling mental illness and that it was the sickness, not his mother, that had rejected him and stolen the love and connection he desired as a child. The most baffling part was that even though he had the acknowledgment of where the abuse came from, like a splinter deep beneath the flesh, the hurt was still there. Now, in his early fifties, this exceedingly successful man sat in a circle of strangers, broken by the words of his mother, who no longer even remembered he was her son.

REJECTION DISTURBS EVERYONE

Consider again how many wounds of rejection a person encounters throughout their life. If you recall, the first section is where you were introduced to the fact that rejection is unavoidable. Rejection still happens even if the person is in the twenty to thirty percent of families who qualify as functional.

These people lived in a home with everything they needed to survive, provided by a robust support system of adults. As they move into adulthood, they anticipate their future, gladly leaving elementary, middle, and high school years behind, where they, too, probably, faced some unavoidable negativity that taints everyone's school-age years. However, that joy is hastily brought to a halt when they realize that rejection seems to always linger around the corner. When they find it in their new job, university, and a fresh circle of peers, it will likely sting them, too.

You would think after understanding that this type of negativity is an inescapable possibility, the functional adult would develop an emotional liberation from the experience of rejection. Rejection hurts, and although perhaps the functional individual learned that the dismissals are not personal, they still feel the initial effects. Yes, even those on the other end of the spectrum with nothing but wonderful things to say about their upbringing and not quite as insecure as the 70 to 80 percent, still cringe at the idea of rejection. The more emotionally healthy we are or work to become, the more our resilience grows. Yet, some types of rejection affect us all, whether one wants to admit it or not.

There is a popular experiment shared amongst those in the field of psychology. Three people sit in a room; two are researchers, and the third is entirely oblivious. He thinks he is waiting to be called in for a different activity that has nothing to do with the one he is unsuspectingly participating in. One of the researchers acts surprised to find a ball on the table and tosses it to the other researcher. The second researcher smiles at the innocent subject and throws the ball to him. Without really thinking about it, the subject tosses it back to the first researcher. After the second round, the gentleman is excluded from the game as the researchers continue to toss the ball back and forth to each other. This study, along with others that used different participants, revealed the same thing again and again. A sense of emotional discomfort rose up in each individual that was rejected by the other two researchers.

You are probably thinking, "How ridiculous!" There are so many other ways of being rejected that are understandably much more painful than not having a ball tossed at you. Plus, the unsuspecting fellow did not even know the researchers. They were outsiders in his life. Yet, the findings of this experiment were always the same. The unsuspecting party, time and again, experienced a low mood and low self-esteem, along with emotional pain.

Remember that we are wired for connection. We have an innate desire to belong and to be accepted. This is true whether we belong to the seventy to eighty percent or the twenty to thirty percent of families.

THE EFFECTS OF VISIBLE AND
INVISIBLE REJECTION

The hard truth, however, is that those who come from a home of dysfunction have lived a life chock-full of rejection grievances. It is quite likely that being excluded from a game involving two strangers, and a ball would cause more significant distress to them than those who have encountered rejection on a more superficial level or less frequently. This is not to downplay the hurt endured by those from well-functioning homes. Of course, they also experience some form of soul distress when facing rejection, but it is assuredly at a lower level of intensity.

The goal here is to shine a light on the toxicity that tends to shroud the adult life of a person who has endured the denial of love and affection or may have felt little to no significance or security during their childhood, the very things every human desires. It is the consistent hurt in their souls from not feeling validated that begins the cycle of destruction for most of these individuals.

If this is you, take a step back and assess your relationships and how you treat those closest to you. Although it may be difficult, you must be honest with yourself. As you ponder the reality around you, look for patterns in your words or actions similar to those that may have caused you distress in your childhood. The obvious rejection can show itself through feelings of anger, hostility, resentment, or dislike, with no real basis behind them. It can reveal itself through physical abuse or insensitive and cruel words. And although not always visibly outright, psychological and physical neglect is also very much a form of rejection.

What needs to be considered are the effects these behaviors have on children and their children's children. Statistics show that kids who witness dysfunctional behavior follow the example they see in their homes and repeat it again when they begin their own families. The Scriptures speak of the consequences passed on from generation to generation. Exodus 20:5 says children are punished for the sins of their fathers. This does not mean that God punishes innocent children, but instead, they will suffer because of the dad's shortcomings.

For example, if a man is self-centered or perhaps prone to drinking alcohol excessively, the child may suffer abuse or neglect as a result. Whether the father is directly guilty of an offense or the state of his drunkenness blinds him to the reality that his child may be enduring abuse at the hands of someone else, that child will suffer.

Anytime the song "Cat's in the Cradle" comes on the radio, my husband gets all teary-eyed. (Sidenote on my husband: I consider him somewhat of an anomaly; he is a tough guy with a very sensitive heart.) He says the song stirs up overwhelming thoughts of his late grandpa and our only son, Jonas.

If you are not familiar with the tune, it's about a dad who is always giving his son empty promises of spending time with him because he is constantly so busy. In the man's old age, when he has finally had the time to slow down, he reflects on all the time lost with his boy and now desires a better relationship with him. He calls his son, but after their conversation, he sadly realizes that his boy is following in his footsteps. He is so consumed with getting ahead that his family has taken a backseat. The last line says, *"And as I hung up the phone it occurred to me, he'd grown up just like me—my boy was just like me."*

Just as good and nurturing behaviors can be passed down, so can unhealthy and destructive behaviors. Showing little to no attention to a child, ignoring their need for comfort or help, spending minimal time with them, or completely ignoring them is indeed rejection. Rest assured, the lack of care and interest in a child will have detrimental effects on their development. Sadly, the likelihood of them repeating the same deeds in their own family is very high.

If you have never taken the initiative or the time to deal with the lingering rejection in your past, an infection of the soul has likely been shoved down beneath the surface. Many will go through their lives convincing themselves that everything is just fine, never entirely understanding the dull ache that seems to signal something is missing.

In an effort to shut off the pain, people will turn to drugs, alcohol, food, sex, or pornography. At times, the things they consume themselves with can look quite normal, even impressive. They will yearn and chase after power and success or attempt to silence the pain by occupying most of their life and energy on their children or careers.

This may sound confusing since I have spent considerable time describing how a child who is emotionally neglected by their parents can cause havoc in their adult life. That still stands. However, here I am referring to a child becoming a placeholder for the pain from the parent's past rejections, and they live their life vicariously through the child. To close the emotional gaps they endured, the parent will invest emotionally in an exaggerated and unhealthy way, where the child becomes the center of their universe.

It is the same with a career, where the person gets an unhealthy sense of self-worth and fulfillment from the success and achievements of their profession. While we all want to be successful, this type can cause the person to ignore other important areas of their life, such as genuine relationships, valuable experiences, and their health.

This is why panic can overwhelm a person who is retiring or sending their children off to college.

All of these behaviors or drives are just coping mechanisms that work to alleviate the disregarded pain. Often, the hurt can unwillingly begin to ooze out, causing problematic distress, such as anxiety or depression. Another destructive consequence of carrying around the invisible wounds of rejection is the tendency to be drawn to others who are in an unhealthy place.

This is why the statistical numbers of dysfunctional families are so high. Not only is the dysfunction passed down from family to family, but it is also multiplied by wounded hearts joining together, bearing the fruit of their combined brokenness through their children. My hope is that you will be the generation that breaks the cycle.

"Blessed is the man who trusts in the Lord, whose trusts is the Lord."

JEREMIAH 14:7 (ESV)

Section 3

THE TRIUMPH

OVER

REJECTION

CHAPTER NINE

BOUND OR FREE: YOU GET TO CHOOSE

"We may not always get what we want, but
we will always get what we choose."

JOHN MAXWELL

S pending the last decade of my life coaching, counseling, and creating content to help people break free from their mental prisons could lead many to believe it was easy to get to this point in my life. Nothing could be further from the truth. I have to confess that my first thirty-three years were spent in a constant spiral of emotional chaos.

During my motherhood years, when I had gathered some wisdom, I learned how to fake the funk when I was mentally falling apart. Which, if I am honest, happened more often than I would like to admit. Even though my life looked pretty well put together to the unsuspecting eye,

I lacked any sense of peace. Although I did not realize it back then, much of it came from what I experienced growing up. It turns out that even if you are born into a home that is in a state of continuous unrest, just because it becomes the norm in your mind, your spiritual nature still knows the difference.

Unintentionally, the turmoil spilled over into my adolescence and adulthood, causing struggles in some of my relationships with others. Like many of you, my search to quell the conflict inside my soul was relentless. Of all the vices I used to relieve the unseen pain, my choice of people was perhaps the worst. They only served to exacerbate my insecurities. This is a reminder that when there is unhealed damage in your soul, believing you deserve the best in life will often be difficult for you to accept. You will say you deserve it, but your actions will show otherwise.

Against the advice of many who loved me, I married at the young age of twenty years old. Back in those days, settling down and starting a family before it was legal to purchase alcohol was widely accepted in my community. Many of my high school friends were getting married or eloping around the same time if they had not already, so it was not a huge deal. The problem was not my age; it was the hasty decision to marry.

THE MADNESS OF COGNITIVE DISSONANCE

I was oblivious to what I was getting myself into when I took the plunge. The abuse came physically and verbally very early on in the marriage, which should not have surprised me since it happened throughout the dating phase. Of course, our insecurities look for countless ways to justify the mistreatment. There was no question that I understood abuse of any kind towards any human being was unacceptable. After all, one of my childhood desires was to find a way to break free from the volatility I grew up in. Somewhere deep inside, I understood this marriage was not the answer, yet I still went through with it.

This is known as cognitive dissonance, a mental conflict between two thoughts that do not match. It happens when we find ourselves acting against things we believe in, which in turn causes discomfort in our souls. To alleviate the discomfort, we lie to ourselves to pacify the battle inside us.

Perhaps the most stupid thing I told myself, outside of believing things might get better, was that at least when I was being physically abused, I fought back. The fact is, I have had numerous conversations with abuse victims who have said the same thing to defend their decision to stay. Like most women in these situations, I foolishly believed taking a vow would change things. And like most women, I could not have been more wrong. In fact, our very first fight was precisely a week after the wedding, and it was worse than any of the ones from before.

During the first year of marriage, I did everything possible to keep my head above the water mentally, physically, emotionally, and financially. Although I will spare you the details, the disconnect and turmoil in the relationship itself should have been enough to make me hit the road. Instead of running away from the situation like any sane person would, I dug my heels in deeper, trying to make things work. Even though, in my mind, I had planned for a happy life of two people, in reality, only one person committed to the journey.

On top of all the fighting, I was so overwhelmed with debt; at one point, I was working three jobs. The old cliché, "The way you do one thing is the way you do all things," fit me perfectly. Like a hamster on a wheel, I was always going, going, going, often at top speeds, but never getting anywhere. After a year of marriage, things got really out of hand for me. I had my car repossessed and lost my home back-to-back.

While you may think that would do the trick and open my eyes to the reality of what was happening, sadly, it did not. Doing everything

I could to prove the naysayers wrong, I chose to endure a tumultuous marriage for much longer than any person should ever be allowed.

VICTIM THINKING

"If only I had known then, what I know now" is something we all have probably said at one time or another. So many things we would do differently. The truth is I was naive, angry, and full of fear in my early twenties. Even worse, I held a very arrogant attitude, so in my mind, the blame fell on everyone else, which meant I did not take too kindly to any manner of advice. My heart was significantly damaged, so I could not receive wisdom in that state of mind. Consequently, "knowing" would not have done any good since I was unwilling to see. Being broken is bad enough, but being broken and blind is a true travesty.

This thought process is known as a "victim mentality" in many of today's circles. You are not born this way; it makes itself at home in your mind due to conditioning and coping with the disappointments and rejections of life. People who struggle with this broken perspective have somehow convinced themselves that others are out to get them and that the life they are living is out of their hands.

Often, they are ready to pounce on the first sign of a threat, as they tend to take offense at most anything. They are prone to personal pity parties, playing the blame game constantly, and always seeing the cup as half empty. Anger from their previous hurts and the fear of even the slightest possibility of the pain happening in the future drive how they see the world around them.

It is an easy mindset to see in others but quite another story to see in yourself. The pain of past rejection fuels this way of thinking. It can rob you of hope for a better future because you cannot get past what happened to you. You become your own worst enemy.

Hear me clearly. I am not suggesting the rejection you have endured is made up or that it is not painful. The reality is you were hurt, and many of you, in unspeakable ways. Whether it happened as a child, an adult, or both makes no difference. The fact that it happened undeniably *made* you a victim, which absolutely will require healing. The key word, however, is "made," the past tense of make.

The truth is that life is difficult, and while it echoes what has already been asserted, it must be restated that you cannot avoid rejection. Humanity is flawed, and humans will disappoint and hurt you. No matter the person, everyone has tasted its bitterness at some point in their life. While the experience levels differ significantly from person to person, we all have the gift of choice.

If you choose to hold on to the hurts and disappointments in your past, you render yourself a victim forever. I cannot emphasize the importance of this fact. If you accept this as your truth for today, you will have surrendered your ability to fight for a better tomorrow. Allowing the wounds of rejection to define who you are will create a paralysis in your mind. This will keep you stuck right where you are, and you will never get healed.

GOD'S NUDGE

Many of the experiences recorded in earlier chapters give perfect credence to what is known as learned helplessness. We subconsciously become so used to the idea that we are powerless that we will give up trying, if we even try at all. If we do make an effort to be better or do better, it usually does not last long. At the first sign of defeat, we crawl back into our cave of weakness and begin making excuses again. Most of us will give in to the "victimized thoughts" and call it quits, reverting back to our old ways.

It was not until I surrendered my heart to my Creator that I began to understand the part that I played in the bouts of pandemonium that seemed to follow me in life. One morning, after my body realized it was all too much to bear, I found myself on my bedroom floor sobbing and pleading for the cloud of hopelessness I felt inside my soul to be removed. Somehow, I knew I had to let go of what was in the past if I wanted to appreciate and live in the present. That was the precious day I encountered Jesus . . . it is a moment that can only be described as divine. God touched my heart so profoundly that day, every time I attempted to share what had happened with someone, I became so flooded with emotion I would break down and cry.

Although I could not put it into words, it was as if I had been granted clarity with my eyes and heart. If I had to describe my new-found vision, I would say outside of the sense of peace and joy I felt, I saw people and the life around me through a lens of love. It may sound corny, but you have to understand before that moment, other than my children, I was the most important person to myself. All of the past rejections had somehow built a callousness in me and around me, so loving others was the last thing on my mind. But that day, something magnificent happened inside of me and changed it all.

There has always been an unrelenting mystery that has continued to eat away at me. *How can two people living through the same scenario have such different outcomes at the end of the day? In other words, why do some break free from the hardship of rejection while others never seem able to outrun it?*

We see the stories of victory from people who have escaped the jaws of painful abuse and neglect as children and become examples of successful, thriving adults for all to see. Yet, countless more succumb to the mental torture of their past. They have unknowingly surrendered to the rejected results of feeling unworthy and unwanted at the expense of a better life.

In other words, without realizing it, perhaps they chose to allow their past to define their future. Maybe they never understood they had a choice. Maybe that is why so many of us have found ourselves in the tormenting grip of life's past rejections. We believed this was just life, never realizing we had a choice. But that is the excellent news, my friend. We have always had the gift of choice.

CREATION

Bear with me as I use a bit of science mixed with sacredness to explain how fortunate humanity is regarding the gift of choice.

If you look around and examine God's creation, you will be amazed by the beauty of what He has given us and by the order of it all. The Hebrew Bible explains that He formed creation and filled it with life within seven days. As described in Genesis, life consisted of plants, animals, and human beings. And while these three forms are incredibly different levels of life, they all have one thing in common: they each miraculously possess a defense mechanism.

Humans are the highest life forms created. However, if you have studied Darwin, you know he claimed humans and animals were one and the same and believed our differences were seen in trivial measures. While there are scientists who, in an effort to avoid the spiritual nature of man, agree with this theory, I most certainly do not.

We are born into this world as a three-part being in the perfect image of our Creator. We are a spirit, that has a soul, and we live in our body. 1 Thessalonians 5:23 points to the tri-part man, *"And the very God of peace sanctify you wholly; and I pray God your whole spirit and soul and body be preserved blameless unto the coming of our Lord Jesus Christ"* (KJV).

The seed-bearing plant is the lowest form of the three life constructs (plants, animals, and humans). Plants are made up of a body, which can reproduce. They also can adjust and acclimate to their natural environment. However, their engagement is limited to the sun, soil, and rain, and only because they need these elements to grow, but they do not possess a soul or spirit. Yet, when issues arise, the plant's body will defend itself against danger.

THE DEFENSE OF A BODY (PLANTS)

Your first thought may be skepticism since this life form cannot move unless it is done through an outside force. However, a quick internet search will lead you to find evidence of just how amazing God's creation is.

A study by the University of Wisconsin-Madison discovered that while a plant does not have a nervous system, like humans and animals, enabling it to feel pain, it most certainly releases a comparable signal, allowing it to respond to attacks or injuries. While a plant cannot run for its life, it turns out that when it is injured, it automatically releases a type of hormone that triggers a healing process, as well as other toxic chemicals that aid in preventing further injury.

THE DEFENSE OF A BODY AND SOUL (ANIMALS)

The next level up is the animal with a body and a soul. They can respond and react to the world in various ways through their body. Their soul allows them to display personality and even show basic emotions such as fear and excitement, but unlike most humans, they have no conviction or sense of morality. While limited, this group has the capacity to reason.

It should be noted it is possible for an animal to surpass the reasoning skills of some humans, depending on the age and development of a person. An example of this would be a primate who learns to communicate through sign language. However, even in this instance, a monkey's mental capacity for reasoning caps at about that of a three-year-old. For this reason, when most animals face danger, although they may have no idea what is happening in the moment, they all at least understand or sense the threat.

Gifted with movement, animals have the choice of fighting it out or fleeing. Some even have innate defense mechanisms, such as a skunk that sprays its enemy or a mimic octopus that changes its color, shape, and behavior to confuse its prey. Whatever option they take is most often an instinctual means of protecting themselves from danger.

THE DEFENSE OF A BODY, SOUL, AND SPIRIT (HUMANITY)

A human also possesses a body and a soul; however, as the most complex of the three lifeforms, he holds something that the other two do not. A person has a spiritual nature that places humanity at the highest level of life. It is this nature that allows us to have a direct connection with God. This connection is developed and reinforced through the worship of the Creator. In other words, by putting God first, our spirit is strengthened.

Additionally, it is through our spirit that we hold the gift of conscience and conviction. Proverbs 20:27 says, *"The human spirit is the lamp of the LORD that sheds light on one's inmost being."* The spirit gives life, holds our true identity, and brings about our purpose.

When a human is threatened, the possibilities for defending themselves are endless. Like plants and animals, reactions to a physical threat may be instinctive or reactive. For instance, when threatened, a person may choose to respond physically or run for cover. However, since we have a soul and are spirit beings, a threat by another person can be dealt with in various ways.

More likely than not, the soul's condition and the spirit's strength will dictate how we react or respond. If one's soul and spirit are healthy and strong, the likelihood of having a good outcome when a threat is posed is high. On the other hand, if the soul and spirit are unwell and weak because they have not healed from the rejections in their life, the reaction will often add more chaos.

SELF-PRESERVATION AT A PRICE

As you can see, all living organisms will avoid that which appears to threaten the very fabric of their being. God's creation is unbelievably astonishing. As the highest level of life forms on the planet, we are not exempt.

Consider this: without any self-effort, a newborn running a fever is actually signaling that something is wrong. At the same time, his immune system is working at fighting off an infection somewhere in his little body. It really is incredible.

However, what makes us stand out above the rest is our need for that which we were born through: connection. As noted in the first two sections of this book, we are born with an innate longing to connect. There is no way around it if we are to function at our highest potential. The feeling of belonging or experiencing a sense of oneness is vital for healthy survival.

For humanity, eliminating or lessening pain and suffering that comes through the many forms of rejection is, at its core, known as self-preservation. The difference between us and the other life forms is that we get to choose how we will defend or protect ourselves. Of course, babies, children, some people with mental disabilities, or emotionally immature adults instinctively react to the rejection in their lives. While they may not realize it, some things occur internally and serve as a means of protection. This happens in numerous ways, and if the rejection faced is traumatic, it may very quickly become part of who they are as they grow up.

For instance, disconnecting and dissociating from people may be what we picked up as a means of guarding ourselves against emotionally or physically unavailable parents. As adults, we have difficulty relating to others, so we self-isolate and convince ourselves that we do not need anyone.

On the flip side, even though these efforts may help to stave off any future rejection, we probably suffer through life with a low-self-image and could have struggles with depression, anxiety, or both. While there is a range of options for humanity to defend themselves against being shunned, mistreated, or feeling threatened, the bottom line is that we often unconsciously do things that tend to alleviate the unpleasant feeling we are experiencing. Even if it is just momentarily.

THE ELEMENTS OF YOU

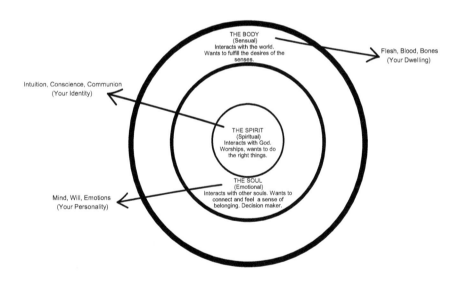

Let us take a closer look at the three parts of humanity-the body, the soul, and the spirit. Imagine a circle made up of three layers. The external layer would be the body, the simplest of the three to describe. It is the carnal side of who we are because we can see it in the reflection of a mirror. It comprises our cells, brain, nerves, and organs. It deteriorates a little every day, so obviously, this part will not last forever. It is the part of us that touches the physical world around us. Our bodies incorporate the senses that allow us to engage in life through five gates: the eyes, the nose, the ears, the mouth, and the sense of touch. It is the sensual part of who we are, as a body seeks to fulfill the desires of the flesh. The Bible refers to this part of our triune being as weak (Matthew 26:41).

The next layer in the circle is the soul. The soul interacts with others, and it exists and desires to belong. The soul constitutes our life as a person and establishes our persona to the world. Some refer to it as our visible personality. In essence, it makes up how others see us, which comes from how we act, react, or speak in situations or to other people.

Our soul is made up of our mind, will, and emotions; this part is responsible for our memories, beliefs, our thinking, values, attitudes, and feelings. Imagine this part as a blank canvas that evolves into a painting of who we are due to our environment. This includes positive and negative experiences, upbringing, education, and culture. In other words, we become who we are through the experiences and life we have lived. The soul is most often the director of the body and the spirit. Since it possesses the will, it is where decisions are made. The will is extremely important to where we currently find ourselves, so we will return to this shortly.

The core, or inner part of the circle, represents our spirit. Our spirit should not be confused with the Spirit of God mentioned in the scriptures, a person also known as the Holy Spirit. Our spirit desires to connect with God and is meant to direct and hold us accountable to the Creator. The spirit is responsible for our reasoning and conscience, intended to drive our judgment of right and wrong. It also guides our intuition and gives us a sense of "knowing" something without any physical or outside evidence. You may have heard people refer to it as the "sixth sense." It is this part of our spirit, I believe, that allows many mothers, and at times fathers, to sense when things are off with their children. Perhaps that "gut feeling" is a bonus parental gift from heaven meant to help us keep our own children in check.

This spiritual nature is the highest level of functioning. The Gospel of John tells us, "It is the spirit that gives life" (6:33). If you recall the story of creation in Genesis, God "breathed life" into the nostrils of Adam. This became the man's spirit, and that spirit brought his soul and body to life. It was that breath that gave Adam life. That is the spirit's first responsibility. The spirit holds the capacity to make us most in God's image (Colossians 3:10). This is where the longing to feel whole comes from, which is why people claim a sense that something is missing. Many refer to it as the "God hole" because the empty space can only be filled by the Creator. It is a personal and strongly held belief that our spiritual nature holds who we were truly meant to be, our true identity. Although God intended for us to be ruled by our spiritual nature, this often is not the case for most of humanity.

"YOU" GET TO CHOOSE

As you have noted throughout these pages, we live in a broken world, and many times, through no fault of our own, we innocently get cut by the sharp edges of other people. The reactions and responses attempt to protect us and come from our soul, either from natural survival instincts or the imitated defenses we saw growing up. Initially, all our soul truly wants is a healthy connection with others and to feel like we belong. After all, we were made for relationships.

Through these connections, the desire is to be loved, accepted, and essentially, to know that we are significant and matter. When our vulnerability brings rejection instead, the soul fends for itself by building walls, creating an unapproachable or unpleasant image, and becoming unusually introverted or exceedingly hostile. The defense mechanism looks different for everyone.

If the truth be told, most of us have done the best we can with what we know to manage this thing called life. Unfortunately, our management skills have likely created even more problems for many of us.

Proverbs 14:12 tells us, "There is a way that seems right to a man, but its end is the way to death" (ESV). In other words, while our soul-ish attempts to protect ourselves from future hurt and pain may make us feel better at the moment, at the end of the day, our outcomes will be futile. With our fists up in the air, we remain ready to take on anyone who portrays an aroma of rejection. It does not matter whether we are looking for a clue of dismissal or disrespect. We will be too busy always looking for the bad and fail to see all the blessings before us. The enemy of our soul has convinced us that everyone is a suspect and no one is to be trusted. Therefore, the anger, insecurity, and loneliness birthed by the rejection that first scarred us becomes stronger, tending to make us more isolated or callous.

If reading this gives you an uncomfortable feeling in the pit of your stomach because it is all too familiar, that is a good sign. Accept and acknowledge the emotions swirling around inside of you. It is simply your spirit nature connecting with your soul, attempting to shed life-giving truth for you. You see, while your soul wants human connection, your spirit is the part of you that God created to connect with Him. Your spirit lets you know this is not how God wants you to live. He never intended for you to live a life full of fear, depression, or anxiety. He wants you to know you are not worthless. He knew you before you were born (Jeremiah 1:5). He numbered your days (Job 14:5), created you with a purpose and a plan in mind, and His intention is for you to prosper (Jeremiah 29:11).

Maybe you ask yourself, "Then, how in the world did I get here, and why do I feel like I will never get out?"

It is simple. Your soul has inadvertently been programmed that way. For many of us, this programming started very early, either by our instinctive defenses or by the words and actions of the people who surrounded us. We learned to kick, scream, or cower to protect ourselves. We made up stories in our heads to make sense of the parent who walked out on us. We grew up listening to the stinging, harsh words of those meant to protect us. We heard things like, "You're worthless, you will never amount to anything, you're just like your father, you're just like your mother, be quiet, no one wants to hear you, you're an idiot, you're a slut, you're lazy, ugly, fat, unlovable."

No matter the choice of insult, it likely and unknowingly stuck. For many of us, it has seeped into the crevices of our hearts, and whether we want to admit it or not, we still believe it to this day. Even when you find yourself succeeding at something, making great strides above the rest, you become paralyzed by the insecurities and thoughts of self-doubt. Understand this: these emotions and beliefs did not appear out of thin air.

AIN'T YOU TIRED?

Just think about it this way. When you see an elephant tied to a small post in the ground, the same thought occurs to most people, "Why does such a massive creature with great indisputable strength not run for freedom when it could very easily tear the post right out of the ground?"

The truth is it stays in place because it was trained to be helpless. When the elephant was a baby and much weaker, it was tied to a similar pole. He probably tugged and tugged, trying to get free, but did not have the strength back then to make the post budge. Eventually, it gave up trying. The elephant, now an adult and undeniably much stronger, remains tied to the pole without a fight because it does not realize that it has more than enough power to break free. He still believes the pole has a hold on him. He has never experienced life any other way, so he has no idea of the magnificence that awaits him if he were ever to taste freedom.

It may seem bizarre, but the same thing happens to us. Do, see, hear, or say something long enough, and it becomes ingrained in your mind. It can actually become part of who you are, even if it is not what God intended for your life. The evidence that you are off the mark of God's plan for you will show up in many ways, but most obviously through a lack of peace.

Perhaps the façade of happiness you portray to the world has become too exhausting to keep up. Maybe your mental arms are tired from holding them in a position ready to fight your next offender. The anger that has comforted you, the isolation that has sheltered you; they do not seem to be enough anymore. If you are not suffering from bouts of uncontrollable rage or stretches of loneliness, it is only because depression and anxiety have taken their place in your soul.

In the Academy Award-winning movie *The Help*, Hilly Holbrook's character masks her internal unhappiness with her external poise and beauty. Underneath it all, she is a miserable and wretched human being. She seethes with anger because the truth of who she truly is has been revealed for the world to see. In an act of vengeance, she lies and accuses Abilene of stealing from her. The iconic words of Ms. Abilene's question to Ms. Hilly say it all. "Ain't you tired?"

While I am sure you are not evil and sinister like Ms. Hilly, I would suppose you may have reached a similar level of misery in your continuous ego-centered attempts to safeguard your heart for so long. The fact that you are reading this book is an indication that the load has simply become too much for you to carry. Know this: it was never meant to be that way.

STOP SETTLING FOR LESS

The truth is that God has given us everything we need to overcome the tricks of torment that have been thrown at us. In the great words of Jesus, "The thief's purpose is to steal, kill, and destroy. My purpose is to give life in all its fullness" (John 10:10, TLB).

According to this scripture, there is an enemy that wants nothing but devastation for you, and it can show up at the hands of another person or through your own personal thoughts. Whether you see this enemy biblically or as the thoughts in your head, the goal is the same: making you believe there are no other options for you. To persuade you that there is nothing more for you and you just need to accept it.

Even worse, you become convinced that you are the only one who feels this way, isolating you further from anyone who will steer you in a different direction. These beliefs will slowly kill your hopes and dreams of doing and becoming who you were meant to be. If nothing changes, you will leave this side of heaven a dismal human being, never realizing your true God-given potential or purpose.

This is why you are where you are now. And it is much simpler than most would have you believe. Like the elephant tied to the post, despite what you have believed for so long, you have the power to break free. In fact, that post does not stand a chance against what God has put inside of you.

Stop settling for less than what God wants for you. You see, you and I have had it all wrong. We have lived life led by our soul and have been deceived into believing that other people's acceptance of us and our accomplishments gave us our worth and value. This is not true.

The deep desire to feel loved, to be accepted, and to know that you matter are His gifts to you. He created you with the need for connection for a reason, and His intention has always been for you to have these desires met. Good-hearted people and all the positive externals we enjoy can be blessings from God because they satisfy our souls. But even they cannot meet the deepest desires of our spirit. The need to feel loved, accepted, and significant were meant to draw us toward a deeper dependency on our Creator. This is the most crucial connection of our life.

The Scriptures lay it out in black and white. They tell us that God is love (1 John 4:16) and therefore He gives us unconditional love (John 15:12) and that His plan for us is to be significant (Jeremiah 29:11) and when we are connected with Him, He will provide us with all of the acceptance our hearts desire (Proverbs 14:26).

All you have to do is choose. Choose life, choose to be set free, choose to live the life of fullness promised to you in John 10:10. Accept the invitation to enter into a genuine relationship with Jesus. He came to earth to empower you to be victorious against all that ails you; the rejection of your past and the toxic defenses of your present have only kept you imprisoned.

Perhaps you sense a certain hesitation. Maybe you think this is true for others, but you doubt this is true for you. You believe you are unworthy. All these are evidence of John 10:10 in your life. So much has been stolen from you without you realizing it. These thoughts live inside your soul as proof of how rejection has led you astray. God loves you in a way that we cannot fathom, as He knew you and formed you before you even took your first breath (Psalm 139:13). He gave you your spirit (Zechariah 12:1) and your purpose (Jeremiah 1:5). And Jesus died so that you could experience that love through His forgiveness and grace. All you have to do is accept it.

THERE ARE NO SHORTCUTS

Can you get through the process of healing and break free without Jesus? Honestly, there are some who claim they have done it. If you do some research on the healing of the soul, I can promise you there will be endless posts, articles, and videos describing steps, secrets, and solutions to this worldwide pandemic of brokenness. Maybe in their minds, they feel they have been liberated. Questioning their reality is not what I wish to do here. I can only speak for myself, and I assure you

I spent years trying all of their ways. While I, at times, received some solace, it was always short-lived.

I attempted to replace the chaos in my soul with other things, creating another version of myself that pretended to not feel the pain of my past. It worked for a little while, at least on the surface. However, like a deep wound covered by a bandage, there was an infection festering beneath that was signaling that something was wrong. When the pain got to be unbearable, I would look to other things to distract me. Just as a pain reliever makes you feel better in the moment, the root of the pain was still there. In an effort to protect me, my soul denied the truth and only helped to delay what God had for me.

So yes, some people claim they have been healed from the rejection of their past with just therapy, or that the hurt they have experienced no longer has a hold of them because of their self-love. I tried those things, too; while the relief came, it was always temporary. I walked around looking okay but never truly had peace. Everything I tried, books, podcasts, and programs, all felt good initially, but in the end, they were superficial.

It was not until I completely surrendered and fully allowed Jesus into my life, trusting Him to set me free, that I began the true process of healing. I gave up trying to do it on my own and decided to go straight to the Source. I allowed my Creator access to my heart; little by little, He began to heal me, giving me a new perspective on almost everything. Each day, I grow closer to becoming who He has created me to be. Perfection will come when I meet Him face to face, but for now I am still constantly learning something new about myself. While not all days are butterflies and rainbows, I would not trade the peace and clarity He has given me for the world.

This is indeed a step of faith and free will. Adam and Eve were gifted with the same free will at the beginning of time in the garden. Like them, you can most certainly reject this invitation. But understand this could mean the poison of rejection will always have a hold on you, and the toxic cycle will continue to exist for you and, quite likely, the generations that will succeed you.

However, if you decide to break loose from the claws of past rejection, the moment you choose to surrender your life to Him, His Holy Spirit comes to dwell inside you and ignite your spirit. Consider this a brand-new beginning (2 Corinthians 5:17), where you will start to discover a new way of knowing the world around you. He will awaken areas in your reasoning, conscience, judgment, and intuition in ways you have not known before. If you choose well, this is just the beginning of a life of freedom!

"The thief comes only to steal, kill, and destroy. I came that they may have life and have it abundantly."

JOHN 10:10 (ESV)

CHAPTER TEN

ESCAPE THE MENTAL PRISON: DISCOVER WHO YOU ARE

"Why do you stay in prison, when the door is wide open?"

RUMI

The greatness of our country comes from the sacrifice of brilliant men who were courageous enough to risk their lives to write and sign the Declaration of Independence. Whether people realize it or not, much is written in this influential document that coincides with Biblical scripture. The foundation of this remarkable text was created by a group of leaders who took a significant risk for liberation. The same can be said about all veterans who fought and continue to fight daily for every American to have this same freedom. This one word is the reason so many people from around the world have the desire to come to the United States of America. Freedom.

Understandably, we have encountered hard times that have interrupted and interfered with this precious gift of liberty. In fact, many question whether we are indeed free. Even then, you have brave individuals who will fight until their last breath to defend the gift of freedom and all it entails. They fight because they have feasted on the sweet taste of independence, and they would rather die than live without it.

The sad truth is that there are those who have never known true freedom for themselves. Even more heartbreaking is that some do not even realize they are bound. Not physically per se, but bound in their soul by the trauma of rejection.

PRISON WALLS

My dearest and closest friend has been a pastor for over a decade and a half. One of the perks of her profession is leading people to the saving grace of Jesus Christ and seeing them set free on an entirely different level. The countless testimonies of people whose lives have been impacted by her perseverance and commitment to her faith are powerful. Like all pastors, however, she did not get to where she is today by osmosis. Considering we have been friends since the age of eleven, I can unequivocally vouch for this fact firsthand.

Her call to serve in ministry came in her early twenties while she was a correctional officer at the local county correctional center. The irony of it all was that it was a group of prisoners who opened the door for her to make that commitment to the Lord.

As the story goes, these men needed one of the county correctional employees to agree to sponsor their weekly Bible study in the facility where they were incarcerated. The sponsor's responsibility was to be present during their meeting time, usually about an hour on a specific workday. She recalls the joy these men had each time she spoke with them, even as she continued to turn down their invitation.

During that period of recent months, she had just gone through a major heartbreak, so she was also facing some rather challenging, heart-rending issues. You may know from your own experiences that the pain from the broken relationship of young love is one of the deepest hurts in the gamut of rejection. It was a pretty difficult time for her.

Yet, these persistent inmates did not let up and continued to appeal to her for help. A couple of months later, realizing she could use the cash from a bit of overtime and something to keep her mind off her emotional struggle, she finally agreed.

FREEDOM BEHIND THE BARS

It was quite a peculiar site. A group of men, serving months and even years of their life without the freedom to go and come as they pleased, filled with so much hope and joy. At first, she just watched and half-heartedly listened, but as time passed, she strangely looked forward to the meetings. After providing support to the group for a few weeks, she became curious about what she was witnessing. My friend had some questions for the gentleman leading the study. How did he hold such a hopeful outlook on life, even as he sat behind bars? Where was all his joy coming from? His response took her by surprise, to say the least.

He explained to her that the criticism and rejection of the world he lived in most of his young life poisoned his heart. It made him bitter, and that bitterness led him down a terrible path. He started hanging with people in the same boat, who unknowingly fueled his hateful perspective on life because they had become slaves to their circumstances, too. He was not proud of the choices that brought him there, behind bars, where almost everything he did was controlled by others.

What he said next somehow shook her, "But I do consider the four walls, fences, and barbed wire I am surrounded by daily a great victory. It is here that I finally have my freedom. The love of Jesus has saved me, His hope has replaced my guilt and shame, and His love has covered my anger and bitterness. And because of His Spirit, I am freer behind these bars than you are out there in the world."

She was speechless. This moment struck up a flame in her soul. I do not know precisely when she surrendered her heart to Jesus, but that moment served two purposes for her. First, it allowed her to take an honest look at where she truly was. Like most of us, the way she looked to the world was masked by something entirely different. While she displayed a strong, stern demeanor on the outside, which ironically was even clothed by an actual authoritative uniform, on the inside was a broken soul filled with discouragement.

Sadly enough, what she carried did not merely come about from her recent failed relationship. Like many of us, her childhood was also plagued by rejection from people who were supposed to give her love and security. The fresh wound of a love gone wrong magnified her childhood's hurts. Like me, and perhaps even you, the choice to enter into such an unhealthy relationship resulted from what she had been masking on the inside of her soul for most of her life. Embracing this truth steered her to the second purpose: a life of ministry that has led hundreds, probably thousands, to an authentic life of Freedom.

FINDING THE TRUE YOU

If you have chosen freedom, as mentioned in the last chapter, you are truly free in your spirit. And while your spirit has been renewed and awakened, you now must willingly do the same for your soul.

The next step is answering the following question: Who are you really? I do not mean the "you" you want the world to believe you are or even the "you" you *think* you are. While that may sound a bit perplexing, the fact is it is possible to lie to ourselves about who we truly are as a person. Firsthand experience taught me this truth as well. When the wounds of rejection have been the internal compass in our soul, we will tend to convince ourselves of many falsehoods.

Jeremiah 17:9 says, "The heart is deceitful above all things, and desperately wicked: who can know it?" Here, the heart refers to the soul part of man, specifically the mind, where understanding and our conscious and subconscious thoughts live. Remember, the soul's goal revolves around safeguarding the "self" and connecting with others. While we want to belong, the soul will always work at protecting itself. Therefore, the soul of a broken individual will construct misrepresentations of how they see themselves. Depending on their natural temperament, this will differ from person to person.

If we are an outgoing person, the mental falsehoods we tell ourselves will often stroke our ego. This personality type may believe they are the next best thing to sliced bread, often disregarding and deflecting from their mistakes. Introverts, those who prefer to be alone, on the other hand, tend to assemble lies on the opposite end of the spectrum. They often see themselves as insignificant and tell themselves they are irrelevant to the conversation. In their minds, they can hardly do anything right.

While these are extreme examples, people with past rejection wounds tend to fall somewhere in between. Both personality types can view or portray who they are as someone grandiose or as a person of little importance; they unintentionally miss the mark. The truth is they do not know who they are as a person, the person God created them to be.

THE DRUG OF APPROVAL: CHECK YOURSELF

We have all been hit by the evil in the world. Rejection has put us in limbo, and we are left either cowering behind our walls of insecurity, afraid to come out, or trying to convince ourselves and others that we are more than what we were made to feel on the inside. Rejection has created internal lies about our worth and value, one way or the other. Whether or not we want to admit it, it has filled us with insecurities.

Of course, the soul's natural desire is to nullify those insecurities. One of its main strategies is through the validation of others. An applicable definition of validation is to recognize, establish, or illustrate the worthiness or legitimacy of something or someone. Actually, to the soul, it makes sense to want to numb the pain of rejection with its polar opposite: approval.

Since we are in an era that is running the world on social media, here is a superficial but straightforward test. Have you ever encountered someone in public who looks entirely different from their last social media post? I am not pointing fingers because I am as guilty as the rest. Those filters give me a boost of confidence, too. If I am being honest, I have had a couple of occasions where posted picture memories pop up on my timeline from when I first joined a platform, and I thought to myself, "Really, Melissa?" To remove my idea of "unacceptable" flaws, the photo was blurred to such an extent it looked like a 2.0 version of an 80s Glamour Shot. I am a work in progress, so please do not judge me too harshly.

Moreover, do you feel the need to excessively post selfies because you find the "likes" filling your approval cup? Now, do not get too alarmed about this question. For the most part, intrinsically, humans want to belong and be approved of. There is actually a science behind the feeling most of us get when someone hits the like button on our posts. The brain releases dopamine, so it automatically gives off a feel-good sense.

The platform creators know this, which means your social media is connected to an internal reward system on purpose. It is designed this way to keep you logged on. The likes can give you a sense of satisfaction and happiness. However, if you are lacking in the area of self-esteem or you dangerously desire to be accepted, these doses of dopamine can create an unhealthy addiction.

Inadvertently, it also soothes feelings of unworthiness while distracting us from our real world. Another red flag is spending extensive amounts of time and effort trying to get this approval high.

THE STAGE OF REAL LIFE

In your real-world encounters, consider the following scenarios. Think about people who come upon a life-altering crisis. Many come out on the other side of the calamity like a different person afterward. If they were who they showed you to be before the event, why do you think there is such a drastic personality change? Yes, I have been there too.

How about personally and professionally? Do you act one way with your fellow employees and another way around those closest to you? I am not talking about how you dress and differences in professional and personal conversations. It is normal to wear a different hat according to where we are. Mom and dad hats on the weekend with our babies, wife or husband hats in the evening, and a professional one during the work week. This question is about masks, not hats. I mean, do you behave better for one group than you do the other? Again, I am not pointing fingers. I was blown away and ashamed, I might add, when God showed me this difference in my life.

In my earlier years, I would walk through the hallways of the building I was working at smiling from ear to ear, like some pageant queen. Everyone I ran into received a resounding and cheerful "Good morning! How are you?" Yet the weekend came around, and I sat around the house with a cringed look on my face that clearly said, "Do not even try to speak to me."

Actually, treating the people at work kindly was not the problem. We should treat everyone with respect. The truth was I was a total jerk to the ones I was supposed to love the most. Sadly, the people at work who offered me nothing more than a paycheck got the best of me.

There was no denying that this revelation hit me like a ton of bricks. I was genuinely shocked; I was putting on a show. But this was a good shock to my reality. I had to get to this place where I was desperate for answers. Desperate enough to choose the path that would free me from the mental prison I had inadvertently built for myself.

The next step was scary. Depending on the level of past rejection in your life, this will probably be difficult for you, too. I had to begin to dig into why I behaved this way. This was the start of my healing journey, and it was probably the hardest for me because I had convinced myself for years that I did not care what others thought about me. Yet, the simple answer to the mask I was wearing, the mask most of us wear, was because somewhere in my soul, I did care, and my wounded soul needed their validation.

AN AWARENESS OF THE TRUTH

Our need to belong and be accepted is part of our natural humanity. Validation, in and of itself, is a normal desire. Remember, we were created for relationships; we long to connect with others. However, when we do not have a solid foundation and rejection comes our way, we conform our true selves to fit what we believe others will like instead.

We have been doing it for quite some time now. Little by little, and unbeknownst to most of us, we lose sight of who we are, constantly bouncing our opinions off of the words of the people we want to impress. This truth is no respecter of persons. Even those we look at in admiration fall prey to the need to impress. It takes more than just looking confident on the outside to be content with everything on the inside and not worry about the opinions of others.

I believe wholeheartedly that our potential and peace of mind come only through knowing our true identity. The more people realize it for themselves, the better they can love those around them, and the more powerful they will become in making their world a better place. Overcoming the effects of rejection is the beginning of this journey for everyone.

We must be aware of who we are to begin to know our true selves. Remember the elephant tied to the flimsy post? Others can see its power and understand that one small step could tear the peg from the ground. However, the elephant has been programmed by its trainers to ignore the power within. We are conditioned by the people we grew up with without even realizing it. As children, we mirror what is around us. We do it because we see the people we look up to doing it.

A child who lives in a home where a parent is being physically abused, yet the abused parent refuses to leave, will be programmed one of two ways. Either they will believe they are powerless and find themselves in similar relationships, or they will run away from anyone who tries to get close because, in their mind, someone may want to pin them down. Both extremes are lies.

The truth is that your true self is not visible to others. In fact, without an intentional sense of self-awareness, it will often not even be visible to you. Your true identity is overshadowed by the hurt, shame, and confusion of past rejection. Your broken emotions dominate who God created you to be. At the end of the day, and without realizing it, the reality is that we are the worst betrayers of our true selves.

Pay attention to the things you say or do in different circles. Do you see a difference? Do you question your words or actions after you have spoken or acted? Does it seem like you use different scripts when speaking to different people? Can you identify times when you have lied about yourself so you would be accepted?

Most of us do not know who we are because we have allowed ourselves to be subconsciously defined by our hurt and pain. This is nothing to be embarrassed or ashamed about.

The things that happened to us, the abuse, the infidelity, the betrayal, the neglect, all of the rejection experiences are who we have convinced ourselves we are. We may not walk around with a sign that says, "Abandoned at Birth" or "Betrayed by My Spouse." Still, at the first indication of trouble, the trauma we experienced will show up as cold and callous, anxious and apprehensive, or any other combination of destructive predispositions. And we convince ourselves that the pain of rejection is who we are when it is simply a result of the heartache that has never healed.

The plans and purpose of our lives are unknowingly swallowed by that pain. Our goal is clear and solid: never let it happen again. That becomes our driving force because if it does happen again, it will reaffirm what we believed in our soul about ourselves the first time we were rejected. "I am unworthy. I am unwanted. I am . . . ," fill in the blank. So, we act accordingly. We say, think, and do what we must and tell ourselves, "This is who I am!"

I hate breaking it to you, but that is not true. While you were created with a particular personality, the plans and purpose behind that personality were not for you to live a life continuously protecting your soul from rejection. Of course, we are to be wise. We should certainly let the suffering of our past be a lesson for our future, but it should not define who we are.

We leave a home, a relationship, or a marriage that has not given us the connection, the care, or the love we were created for behind. But because the pain of the rejection has seeped inside us, into the deep crevices of our soul, it goes with us wherever we go. We think we are free when, in fact, everything we see is through those lenses.

This does not by any means make you a fraud. It is your soul's way of managing life and protecting you. It is actually your soul that has

138

convinced you that you are your memories, your profession, your appearance, your associations, your family history, and on and on. They may all affect how you behave and what you believe, but it is your spirit that knows your true identity.

Jeremiah 29:11 was my saving grace when I was deep in a pit of depression. In my early thirties, I had worn myself ragged, trying to impress the world and prove to myself that I was someone. All the turmoil of my childhood, the mental suffering of failed relationships, and the disconnection I had with my husband back then were numbed by the massive schedule I was keeping. Working a forty-plus-hour week and going to school full-time while juggling two children, a husband, a home, and homework assignments was taking its toll, but I dared not slow down for fear that someone would deem me a failure. I had to keep up with the façade.

My poor body was stressed out by the load of responsibilities I willingly and proudly carried; my mind was clouded by the lack of sleep. So worn out it was no surprise when I caught the flu right after the Christmas holiday. However, the worst part was not the aches and pain; it was the shock my whole being (body, soul, and spirit) experienced when I was forced to be still.

While I did not realize it at the time, the jolt of immobility opened the door for every single issue I had been working so hard to pretend did not exist to come to the surface. The gush of emotions came rushing through like a broken dam, overwhelmed by prolonged periods of rain and flooding. Except I would equate my rainstorm to the one in the days of Noah. It had been a long time coming.

For most of my young life, the painful feelings that came from a rejected and broken heart filled my mind with lies. Instead of feeling and acknowledging the emotions, I pretended not to care. I told myself I was strong and perfect just by myself. My mind's solution was to detach from my feelings and become callous enough to go through the motions of life without anyone noticing. No one did, not even me.

ANGER TURNED INSIDE OUT

They say depression is anger turned inside out. I would have to agree. The emotion can arise from feeling a lack of control when things turn out differently than we would have wanted. It often comes as a reaction to either an imagined or genuine injustice. It can be denied or stuffed by not acknowledging it, but it is still there no matter how much we want to act as if it does not bother us. What I know now that I did not know then is that you can only pretend that you do not care for so long. It is the pretending that covers who we were truly meant to be.

There is nothing wrong with feeling angry. Jesus got angry and overturned the tables when certain individuals were defiling and making a mockery of God's temple (John 2:13–18). It is a God-given emotion meant to help us deal with problems. When we feel it rise up because of the injustice of rejection against us but fail to acknowledge, understand, and process it, we will eventually have problems. If our pride pushes us to act as if we do not care, or even worse, allow it to produce bitterness in our hearts, there will be destructive consequences sooner or later.

Not only unaware adults suffer from the backlash of these suppressed emotions. As children, we cannot fully understand the chaos we are experiencing emotionally. A child will unknowingly develop emotional tools to survive, and often, as an adult, they can be detrimental to them and those they say they love. In either case, young or old, the mind has absorbed all the hurt from the rejections, unconsciously recording it in the soul. The emotions or reactions developed to protect the soul from those same hurts create a governing idea of who people believe they are.

This effect is considered trauma, which happens inside someone due to such painful events. At some point, the individual must decide to work through the trauma, or it will keep a person stuck in the past.

If it is not addressed, they will continue to believe they are who they are because of what they have endured. Additionally, it will rob them of the pleasures and blessings in life. However, it must be acknowledged first.

REMOVE THE MASK

Choosing to be free from the poisonous effects of the rejection of your past was your first step. The next step involves unmasking yourself. This means admitting that somewhere along life's journey, you subconsciously chose to masquerade the true you. This will not be an easy feat for a couple of reasons. If your rejection came at a young age, and you have done your best to put it behind you, you may struggle to get to the truth. Furthermore, if you have prided yourself on what others think of you, and fear has driven you to be someone you are not, you will have to overcome the fear of judgment.

Yet if you have chosen freedom and desire the will of God for your life, the Book of Psalms will speak directly to this dilemma. Verse 56:11 reads this way, "In God I have put my trust, I shall not be afraid. What can mankind do to me?"

If you have surrendered your heart to God, people's approval should no longer be the most important thing in your life. We cannot live a full life, always concerned about what others may think of us. If you put God first, whatever they think of you is not your business. This is a hard pill to swallow, especially if your whole life has revolved around creating a certain idea of yourself for others. A good reminder I used to overcome this mental battle was that at the end of the day, I was responsible for myself, and other people did not pay my bills. It may sound cheesy, but it has worked for me.

On the contrary, God will supply all your needs according to his riches (Philippians 4:19). Make it easy for yourself and put your trust in the hands of your Creator instead. He loves you unconditionally and beyond human comprehension. He is love (1 John 4:8), and what you think of yourself or what others have done to you does not matter. He loves you because of who He is, and you cannot do anything to lose or earn His love. You simply have to receive it.

Allow His perfect love to make you feel safe without the mask and amid your imperfections. Relax and let His Spirit show your spirit the genuine confidence that comes from trusting Him with all of you.

You need to grab hold of the reality that your early experiences, especially those that did not give you the connection and love you were created to receive, have established false ideas of the true you in your soul. You have willingly decided you want to be set free and have accepted Jesus by faith. Restoration from the lies you have believed for so long is what you need (Romans 12:2).

Understand that God created you to be you and not someone else. Not someone who shrinks back from humanity to hide and never be hurt again. Not someone who has grown cold and callous towards society, suspicious and ready to fight everyone. Both of these are rejecting the real you. God has an abundant plan for your life, but in order to take hold of it, you must uncover what is hiding beneath the mask.

Find a quiet place by yourself where you can spend some time meditating on the journey that has brought you to where you are today. It is time to open up your soul; your mind, will, and emotions to God. You are going to have to give your ego a break and lay your pride down. You will have to lay down your fears and come out of the cave you have created for yourself.

Pray for the courage to lay the mask down. Ask for insight into why you picked up the mask in the first place. What parts of you were you attempting to hide? What parts of you are God-given and true? What God-given parts of who you truly are have been tainted by the rejection of your past? What parts of you have been established as a way to protect yourself from future rejection?

It is in this place where if you are open and genuine, He will begin to do a work in your soul that will move you towards being who you were truly created to be.

But the fruit of the Spirit is love, joy, peace, forbearance, kindness, goodness, faithfulness, gentleness and self-control. Against such things there is no law.

GALATIANS 5:22-23

CHAPTER ELEVEN

CULTIVATE THROUGH THE CALLOUSNESS: FIND FORGIVENESS

"A good tree cannot bear bad fruit, and a bad tree cannot bear good fruit."

JESUS, MATTHEW 7:18

The inevitable sting of rejection may not touch all of us equally, but it does touch us all somehow. The bottom line is that if we are part of the seventy to eighty percent unsuspectingly impacted by a dysfunctional individual or family, the effects for you are much more profound. You probably carry a root of rejection that seemingly produces or has produced, in the past, unwanted fruit in your life. The consequences to the individual who has experienced trauma due to their family dysfunction or at the hands of a careless individual will undoubtedly have more negative life outcomes than some may want to admit.

THE ANALOGY OF A TREE

Like all living things, the tree sprouts forth from a seed. This seed has an outer coat that protects the embryo and holds the endosperm, a food reserve for future growth. The embryo is a tiny plant inside, lying in wait for just the right time to feed off the nutrients of the endosperm. The protective coat seems to know when it is safe for the seed to grow. When the natural environment, which includes the amount of water, temperature, and light, is just right, the seed begins to germinate or sprout, and the roots pop out and begin to journey downward.

Once the roots make their debut, they begin to pull water, oxygen, and vital minerals from the soil to the tree. The roots create a path for nutrients from the soil to the seed and hold it anchored in the ground to keep the tree growing properly. While they are hidden underground for the duration of the tree's life, they are the most crucial part of the tree. You see, without roots, the tree cannot survive.

At around the same time, the seed is pushing upwards towards the light in an effort to sprout leaves and become a seedling. With the right temperature, the seedling continues to grow bigger and stronger, becoming a sapling and then a tree. As a tree, it will soon produce seeds of its own through the creation of good fruit.

Like people, the seed type will determine the tree type. While unseen, the roots of a tree make up approximately fifty percent of that tree, making them very important to its health. It turns out that the better you understand the root system of a tree, the healthier it will

grow. Remember, the roots pull water, oxygen, and vital minerals from the soil to the tree and keep it secured in the ground and growing properly.

To avoid any damage to the root system, there should be an effort to maintain a healthy and resilient environment around the tree, as well as always being careful to prevent the soil from being highly compacted. If there is damage or injury to the root system, dieback will occur. Dieback is easily spotted through dry, dead patches of leaves on the tree. It will be visible in individual limbs or branches depending on where the damage in the root system is and, in some cases, on the type of tree.

VICTIM MENTALITY

The human soul, infected with a contaminated environment of rejection, similar to that of a tree, will create a kind of root system that permeates the individual's life, reflecting the corruption in what it produces. Instead of dead leaves, it will show up through fear, unhappiness, and hopelessness, at the very least. These people may find that they are simply surviving from day to day, never really being able to enjoy the gift of life. Everything around them is seen through the root of their rejection.

A person with a negative disposition, wherever they go, leaves a trail of criticism and pessimism behind them. Consider these types of disposition as bad fruit. These people are never really able to create genuine friendships. Perhaps, worst of all, the roots of rejection have produced an outlook of victimhood. This is where a person never takes responsibility for the life they are living. It is a dangerous place to find oneself, and one of the perspectives I often encounter when working with people who say they want to be free.

As we have repeatedly noted in past chapters, the world we live in can be harsh and unfair to people; almost everyone can confirm this. It is also important to mention again that it is probably true that much of our suffering has happened at the hands of others and often through no fault of our own.

You may say, "That sounds like we are victims to me." And you are correct. Whatever your experience of adversity was, the fact that you were powerless to do anything about it made you a victim. However, just because you were a victim during your experience or experiences does not mean you have to stay that way.

Adopting this mentality creates a bad seed of resentment. When it begins to grow, it produces a root system that will deliver bad fruit. As a result, anyone who comes in contact with this person will likely suffer.

As a former victim, your innocence from wrongdoing should free you from guilt. You also have the right to feel whatever comes up inside you, but do not allow the feelings to make themselves at home or lead you. More importantly, understand that as soon as you blame the other person for where you are in life, you have surrendered your power. While the anger some victims feel inside will create a sense of power, it is a façade.

Just turn on your nightly news, and you will see this play out on the world stage. This following statement may not be politically correct, but it is true, and I stand behind it wholeheartedly. An entire global arm thrives and depends on people believing they are a victim by painting scenarios and developing narratives that stir up intense emotional reactions. Governments and several movements disguised as advocacy groups for social justice fall into this category. They either solidify their power or pad their pockets with those who buy into the victim mentality they are selling. The fruit that it produces, although it may initiate from a good place for some, is more often than not divisive and bitter.

Look real closely. As long as you feed into the idea that it is someone else's fault that you are where you are, you will cease to take action for yourself. While I am sure many groups are genuine in their cause, the point is to highlight the process of paralysis that takes place in the minds of those entranced by someone else's vow of vindication for them.

When it comes to these "heroic" parties, they promise to be your champion, and at some point in the future, they will save you from the hooks of those who dare bring injustice to your doorstep. They string you along, with tiny victories here and there, while you do nothing but wait for them to rescue you.

This is similar to what happens when we hold grudges and are mad at the world, maybe without even realizing it. While our pain may be real, and we were victims of past rejections through betrayal, manipulation, abuse, or other prior traumas, we cannot stay there. Remember, as humans, we tend to find ways to protect ourselves from future pain if possible. Blaming someone else and staying stagnant is the easiest way to do this. We must learn to be kind to ourselves, release the other person, and give ourselves permission to move forward.

Since we have now determined to take our masks off and allow God to show us our true selves, this next statement may be confusing. Moving into this next level of freedom can be difficult because many individuals are blinded to their reality. Just as the tree's roots are not visible to the naked eye, neither is the source of the unforgiveness deeply seeded in our souls. For some, it is pretty straightforward, and we know we hold unforgiveness. But for others, something just feels off inside.

We convinced ourselves that the emptiness can be filled with meaningless stuff, the critical attitude is somehow part of who we were meant to be, and everyone in our life is to blame for what goes wrong. There is a root somewhere that produces the emotions that steal your peace, and we need to find it.

LET'S TAKE A LOOK AT OUR FRUIT

Just as we were willing to take off the mask, we now have to be honest about the painful fruit that has robbed us of living a full life. The root causes of unhealed rejection and the trauma that is sometimes associated with it can unknowingly change the trajectory of our lives.

Find a quiet spot when you have about ten minutes to focus on this next section without interruptions. You will read and check any of the boxes that apply to you. Understand that your soul will want to protect you, so you will be inclined to object. Initially, you may not recognize or wish to accept some of the disguises that hide the destructive roots that have been hindering you from truly living your life in freedom. Just as we did with the mask, you must be determined to be absolutely sincere with yourself.

Our goal is to reveal if there is a root of rejection so that we can take the necessary actions to remove its power and begin to heal our souls. Just as a patient with an unknown cause of pain will be honest about their symptoms with the doctor, you will do the same with yourself and God, the Grand Physician.

Reader's Note

You want to be mindful that biological factors such as fluctuating hormones, high-stress levels, lack of sleep, and physical health issues can affect your emotional well-being. As you explore and meditate on the list, you want to identify patterns, consistent beliefs, and behaviors that are part of your characteristics.

Self-Reflection

Read the following descriptors to see if any of these characteristics describe you.

❑ You are a highly sensitive individual whose feelings are easily hurt. You misinterpret the words and actions of others as a rejection of who you are. You anticipate being overlooked, thus refraining from attempting to participate in conversations or events. If you do participate, it is usually after much encouragement or pleading from others. The wounding from your past may even cause you to isolate yourself in an effort to protect yourself from being hurt in the future.

❑ You mentally prepare to expect negative responses from others before you even approach a group of people or an individual. This outlook causes you to take constructive advice as criticism. You see people's intentions towards you as an attempt to hurt you, even when they simply want to help.

❑ You tend to become angry or defensive when someone questions you. It is difficult for you to have a productive conversation and build relationships because a question the other person poses can be seen as an attack on you personally. It is as if you are ready to fight and defend yourself at every turn.

❑ You tend to be highly argumentative, constantly feeling that you need to be right in every situation. The necessity to be right is a way of validating who you are to re-establish the self-worth stolen from you during the rejection period in your life.

❑ You are a people pleaser, always on the hunt for approval. The danger in this characteristic is that you do not know how to say no and bend to every whim, often feeling overwhelmed. You wrongly believe that saying yes to everyone will keep you from future rejection when, in fact, it can open the door for selfish people to use you. On top of your tendency to please people, you overrate the praise of others. In fact, insignificant disapproval that most people will brush off may cause you to be consumed by their words or gestures or, at the very least, become inundated with worry and doubt, questioning your abilities and self-worth.

❑ You have an extreme love for attention. This one is harder to recognize since most people want to be noticed in some way or another. This is more than fishing for compliments, although if you find yourself almost forcing others to point out the things you want to impress upon them, it may also be an issue. The toxicity of this type of attention-seeking is seen through two extremes.

- The first is an overtly aggressive and loud expression to prompt an agreement from someone else.

- The second seeks sympathy continuously or feigns a lack of ability often. People may identify you as a "drama queen or king" who always tries to get noticed.

Both ends of the spectrum attempt to cover the lack of attention endured earlier in life.

❑ Your mood changes erratically, almost as if swinging from a pendulum. One minute, you are joyful, and the next, you are crying or angry. These erratic changes come as responses to veiled wounds in your soul that you do not realize are there. Due to the unsuspecting injuries that have infected your soul, you will find it easy for the people around you to influence abrupt changes in your mood, too. On that same note, if you find yourself in a position of management or supervision, you will be inclined to lead with an iron fist to cover up your insecurities. Often, your position is filled with growing complaints from subordinates, causing you to lose the job or quit before you have to face the rejection of being let go.

❑ Your intense fear of failure and rejection causes you to avoid risks and make excuses when presented with opportunities to step outside your comfort box and attempt something new. You evade positions that require you to lead others or take responsibility for noteworthy positions or situations. This creates mental anguish inside of you. The voice in your head is constantly questioning your worth.

DIG A LITTLE DEEPER INTO YOUR SOUL

If you have identified with any of these descriptors, there is a high indication that rejection is deeply rooted in your soul. While we are free in our spirit by God's amazing grace when we accept Jesus, we need to be set free in our souls and forgive those who have rejected us. When you chose to be set free, you decided you wanted to live your life abundantly and detached from the grips of your past hurts. But let me be clear: those hurts also include the ones you have created.

If you are anything like me, some of the failings in your life were your own doing. If you are going to continue to move forward, you need to hand those over first. The freedom that Jesus brings when you accept Him comes from His grace and forgiveness for all your short-comings.

We are often the hardest on ourselves, carrying humiliation and a sense of unworthiness deep in our souls. Ironically, the shame we hold onto because of something we have done in our past causes us to be our own biggest rejecter.

What is essential to understand is that living with a masked identity comes with confusion, uncertainty, low self-esteem, an inability to connect, and many other negative emotions that lead us to do and say things completely out of our God-given character.

Thinking about yesterday's destructive words and actions may not feel good, but you must understand two things. Romans 3:23–24 tells us, "For all have sinned and come short of the glory of God; being justified freely by His grace through the redemption that is in Christ Jesus" (KJV).

First of all, this clarifies that none of us is a perfect human being. We all have faults and have failed. You are not alone. Secondly, and the good news, God provided the perfect solution for all of our short-comings by sending Jesus to die for our sins. Through His sacrifice on the cross, we are forgiven and justified by God's grace. It is a gift you receive by faith when, through self-examination, you come to realize that the life you were living was based on deceptions.

Take a moment alone, and ask the Holy Spirit to reveal anything you are holding against yourself. Ask Him to uncover sins you have committed that you may not realize are holding you hostage.

Digging deep is not easy when it comes to our soul, but if you do not follow through with excavating your deep-seated self-inflicted wounds, they will only keep you trapped as you move forward.

God's forgiveness is for all of us, and receiving it allows us to move forward into complete restoration. It is always your choice, but remember Jesus came to save us from our sins, which is something we cannot do for ourselves. Confess them to Him; He already knows them. Accept your own forgiveness, and give over anything you have been holding against yourself.

"In Him, we have redemption through His blood, the forgiveness of our trespasses, according to the riches of His grace" (Ephesians 1:7 ESV)

Just as you chose freedom for yourself, God chose to forgive you and me. He did not have to, and while we believed we were unworthy of His forgiveness, He gave it freely. So, this next part may sting a bit, or a lot, if you are anything like I was before Jesus, but it will be worth it.

However, if you want to take the power away from the rejection of your past, you cannot miss this next step. If forgiveness was difficult to receive, it will be just as hard to give, but it does need to be paid forward. After you have accepted His forgiveness, it is time for you to consider giving the same forgiveness to those who inflicted pain on you through the rejection of your past.

WHAT FORGIVENESS IS NOT

If you are like most people, the thought of forgiving those who have caused you pain can leave you feeling a bit confused and, at the very least, apprehensive about taking that step. The reasons for hesitation are understandable. After all, the rejection you endured, no matter what it looked like, changed the trajectory of your soul.

It is the unforgiveness that produced feelings of hostility, resentment, fear, stress, and bitterness inside of you, all in an effort to protect your soul against those who were supposed to love and care for you. These negative feelings created a false sense of power that has crippled you in areas of your life, slowly destroying your well-being. Essentially, eating away at your peace like cancer without you even realizing it was happening. It has likely limited the enjoyment of healthy relationships. The saying, "Unforgiveness is like drinking poison and hoping your enemy will die," is spot on.

It is, in fact, not the rejector but the denial of forgiveness towards them that has kept us tied to the post. Why, then, do people refuse to let go of something that only serves to harm them?

Personally, I believe it is because there are many misconceptions around forgiveness. Forgiveness does not mean that you accept the wrongdoing of rejection in your life. Forgiveness does not mean you dismiss or deny what has happened to you. Forgiveness does not require reconciliation, nor does it mean the offender needs to repent or apologize for the pain they have caused you, even if that is what you desire.

Despite what many think and how empowered the anger behind unforgiveness feels, forgiveness does not signify weakness. In fact, it is one of the most valuable and strong actions a former victim will ever take.

Forgiveness can be uncomfortable, especially if you were expecting the other person to pay for what they did. Fundamentally, you are canceling what you believe they owe in return for more freedom. Forgiveness gives you permission to move forward with your life by not allowing the rejection of the past to hurt you any longer. It will take the power away from the offender and begin the process of healing your soul. This, in turn, will draw you closer to the One who has already forgiven you.

CULTIVATE FORGIVENESS

You have decided to choose freedom by surrendering your heart to Jesus. You trusted Him to guide you as you laid down your mask to uncover the real you. Now, to follow through with the process of healing your soul, you need to get to the real root of the rejection, which has managed to steal your joy and peace, at the very least. If you have been walking around with a rejection wound for some time, you have a deeper root to deal with.

Once you figure out where the issues lie, you can forgive both the offense and the offender. Remember, God will not force you to forgive. Just as you willingly chose His gift of freedom through a relationship with Him, you must do the same with forgiveness. At this point, you may not be able to fathom the idea of letting your offender off the hook for what happened to you. If so, it makes sense because your soul wants to keep protecting you. It may take some time to get to the point where you decide you are ready to move forward and begin forgiving those who have hurt you, which is okay.

Something that will prepare you and open the door for your spirit to lead you to the next step is prayer. If this is new to you, or your mind is having difficulty moving into forgiveness, this will be a bit strange. One of the most well-known prayers around the world comes from the Bible. It is the moment that Jesus gives the Sermon on the Mount and teaches His disciples how to pray. The prayer in Matthew 6:9–13 goes like this:

"Our Father, who is in heaven, hallowed be Your name; Your kingdom come; Your will be done on earth, as it is in heaven. Give us this day our daily bread. And forgive us our debts, as we forgive our debtors. And lead us not into temptation, but deliver us from evil" (NKJV).

This will not become a lesson in the Lord's Prayer, but there are a couple of things that may cause hesitation for some that must be noted here.

First, the words "Our Father" are meant to connect us with God as His children. If the rejection offense was paternal and came from your father or a father figure, your soul may have trouble receiving this truth. Your mind will immediately want to compare your earthly dad to the Creator of the Universe. I know this to be true because I had the same struggle.

If your father happened to be cold and distant, you may imagine that God is not interested in you. If your dad was abusive in any way, you may have difficulty trusting God at all. Perhaps you were abandoned or lost your father early on; you may find it hard to believe He even exists.

Let me assure you, even if you were one of the lucky ones, and your father was caring and patient with you, you may have a better idea of who God is, but there is still no comparison to the Father in this prayer.

All these beliefs are based on deceptions developed from your own experience, good or bad. The reality is that God is the definition of a father. He is the Creator of the created and loves us unconditionally and inexplicably. He is a Father to the fatherless (Psalm 68:5), and He will never fail you.

Your spirit will have to take the lead here. Romans 8:15 tells us that we received God's Spirit when He adopted us as his own children. Remember the identity you discovered in the last chapter. Who you believed you were was based on the lies of rejection when, in fact, your perfect Heavenly Father sees you for who you truly are and calls you His masterpiece (Ephesians 2:10).

It is hard to understand that there are no fiery hoops you need to go through to receive His love and position as a child of God. You simply must believe and receive it through faith. I promise you it is the only way, which leads to my second note.

In the prayer, Jesus calls us to forgive those who have offended us, just as our Father has forgiven us. We are asked to forgive as we have also been forgiven.

While we may be outstanding people in our community, loving parents or spouses, good employees, or employers, we are not perfect. In the first section of this book, attention is drawn to the fact that we all play a part in the patterns of rejection in some way. If we are honest, which we want to be, we probably take out our frustrations and pain on those we call family and friends from time to time. Maybe we are not directly or intentionally rejecting our people. However, we can withhold love, commitment, and communication from those meant as blessings in our lives.

Understand this: suppressing or refusing to connect with the people closest to you is part of what is stealing your joy and peace. It is a symptom of your unforgiveness, and it is keeping you from experiencing the abundant life meant for you. You should not only forgive because you were forgiven; you should forgive because it continues to cause disconnection in your relationships and destruction in your soul.

Praying the prayer in Matthew will draw you close to God, which will begin to change your perspective and soften your soul. Take all the time you need, but be reminded that there is an overwhelming sense of peace that awaits you on the other side.

IT IS TIME

When you are ready, set aside time and start with a journal or piece of paper to create a list. Consider the person or persons who have rejected, neglected, ignored, or abandoned you. This will be uncomfortable for many of you because your soul has fought for you to avoid the subject altogether, perhaps causing you to seethe in anger anytime the thought comes up. You want to sit quietly and ask God to bring them to mind. For some of us, the list is short: one or two people. For others, it will be lengthy, either because we have succumbed to a spirit of offense or our contrived defense mechanisms, amid rejection, have made way for consistent rejections to follow us around. Neither is right nor spiritually healthy.

Once your list is set, start with the first person and recall the actual offense against you. You can do it mentally, or you can write it down. Either way, you want to acknowledge the hurt and pain that came with the experience. Note the emotions that rise up, both at the time of the offense and now. What, in your mind, did that offense tell you about who you are?

Some examples might be, "When my father left me as a child, I felt ashamed for not being good enough and have spent most of my life trying to be perfect." "When my uncle abused me sexually as a child, I felt shock and shame and have thought of myself as unworthy most of my life." "When my girlfriend cheated on me, I felt rejected, and it has caused me to be angry towards others."

If you still find yourself a bit hesitant, consider this reminder about the person who transgressed against you. People who hurt us, whether through verbal and physical abuse or neglect and abandonment, have likely endured abuse themselves. The abuse they experienced impeded their ability to connect in meaningful or healthy ways. This does not make their rejection okay or remove any blame for their actions. However, it brings some clarity and credence to the effects of almost seventy percent of families living in dysfunction. Understanding this truth can help as it will work to break the cycle of dysfunction. It also gives you a starting point for forgiveness.

The life and death of Jesus illustrate this truth. He experienced rejection to the point that He hung on a cross (for us) because of it. I can imagine Jesus looking down from the cross. He watched the soldiers gambling for His clothing, the leaders of the religious community mocking Him, and the people who once were thrilled by His presence blaspheming His name as He took His last breaths.

Every single last person around Him was unworthy of what happened next. He looked up into heaven and prayed to God for them, saying, "Father, forgive them for they know not what they do" (Luke 23:34). He was not condoning their actions. They all would someday have to give an account for their sins even if they misunderstood the blessing He was in their life. He was their redeemer, yet their sinful hearts were blind to the truth.

While you are not God, this is essentially what happened to you. People oblivious to the blessing you were meant to be in their life rejected you. Some even may have rejected you because of God's protection over you. There really is no way to know. But one thing is certain: the rejection of your past does not change who you were meant to be. God has plans of peace and joy for your future. Ask Him to help you forgive so you can be completely free. Take the first name on your list and repeat this prayer or something similar aloud:

Lord, I believe you want me to be fully restored in spirit and soul. I ask you me heal from the hurt of rejection that was inflicted upon me. As you have forgiven me, I forgive (name the offender) for (name the offense). Help me to remember your truth about me, and drive out the lies in my heart. Just as I have surrendered my life to you because I chose to walk in freedom, I surrender this situation to you as well, Father.

You want to do this individually with each person on your list. You may want to do it more than once with some individuals, if you need to. While forgiveness is not a feeling, you will sense a weight lifted off you after genuinely forgiving. However, be aware that your memories are still there, but remember, they are simply memories that cannot hurt you.

As the memories come up, ask God to fill the negative thoughts with His truth about you. You are loved, connected to, and accepted by your Heavenly Father. You have been created in His image (Genesis 1:27). He has a plan and purpose for your life (Jeremiah 29:11). If you allow Him, and continue to depend on Him, He will continue the process of taking the pain and emptiness caused by the damaged roots of your past and will begin to do a new thing in your soul. He will bring life to the places that were dry and restore the places that were diseased.

See, I am doing a new thing! Now it springs up; do you not perceive it?
I am making a way in the wilderness and streams in the wasteland.

ISAIAH 43:19

CHAPTER TWELVE

THE REJECTION RESOLUTION: START WALKING

Jesus told him, "Stand up, pick up your mat, and walk!"

JESUS, JOHN 5:8 (NLT)

In the heart of Jerusalem, a man who could not walk had been lying by the pool of Bethesda for an excruciating thirty-eight years. The power behind this remarkable story comes as Jesus enters the scene and speaks directly to this invalid. Keep in mind that the word invalid carries a profound meaning—a person who is made weak or disabled through illness or injury. Around the pool was a collage of human suffering, people who were blind, paralyzed, lame, and sick. All burdened by the weight of their pain, all yearning for a miracle.

In this chronicle, the people believed that an angel would come to stir the waters and that stirring was like no other because it brought

163

complete healing to people. But the healing was only for the person who entered the pool first. This meant that there was only one winner per day, so to speak, and if you were too slow, you were out of luck for a healing.

Jesus approached the man lying there for years and asked if he would like to be made well. The man's response was not what one would expect when presented with the possibility of complete physical restoration. My guess is most of us believe we would give a resounding, "Yes! Please tell me what to do."

Instead, the man in the story begins to explain, or rather complain, that he has no one to help him in the pool. And that someone always beats him to the punch. We can only imagine what life must have been like for this man up to that point. He had given up on himself; he depended on someone else to assist him with everything, including the possibility of being set free. Naturally, he was full of excuses.

If you can, for a moment, think about the parallels between the thoughts and the life lived by this physically crippled man and the thoughts and life of a person suffering from the impact of repeated rejection. Both have lived for so long with a defeated mind; they are frozen by doubts and find it hard to believe there is a better way.

Jesus dismisses the lame man's justifications but does not shun him. The question remained: did he want to be healed? This is significant because Jesus could have instantly healed the crippled man without saying a word, but that is not what happened here. After the man lists his excuses, Jesus heals and tells him, "Stand up, take up your mat, and walk."

This directive is as meaningful and powerful for us as it was for the disabled man who lay by that pool. As you move into the other side of rejection and through to complete healing, you will see both the question and the command are key to breaking completely loose from the grips of past rejection, staying victorious in your freedom, and living a life of restoration.

CHOOSE TO ADMIT THE TRUTH

When I first read this story, I thought it was strange to ask someone who is crippled if they want to get well. In my mind, if I had been debilitated for almost forty years, of course, I would want to be made well. Who would not want that? However, through many years in ministry and coaching, I have come to the realization that not everyone does want to get well. The truth is some people have grown so comfortable in their defeated way of thinking they do not even realize they are mentally paralyzed.

Misery has become their modus operandi, and that is how everyone knows them. Everyone but themselves. There are others who do realize they are in a cycle of destruction but are afraid of what it will take to come out of the cave of rejection they have come to accept as home.

Then there are some who either realize it and will say their desire is to be made well. They find comfort in the support and attention they receive from those trying to help, but they always go back to square one because the discomfort is too much for them to bear. Others still have settled into their helplessness, and whether they recognize it or not, they sadly crave the attention it brings them.

What we need to understand is that when Jesus posed the question, he knew the crippled man's heart condition.

In the book of Genesis, the Bible says their eyes were opened after Adam and Eve ate the forbidden fruit. In other words, the bite of the fruit caused them to lose their innocence, so when they understood they were naked, they covered themselves with fig leaves. Then, when they heard God walking towards them, knowing what they had done, they hid from Him. Even though God knew where Adam was, He called to him and asked, "Where are you?" (Genesis 3:1–10).

If God knew the condition of the man's heart who lay by the pool of Bethesda and the man's location in the Garden of Eden, why did he ask a question He knew the answer to? Simple. There had to be accountability from them. They had to take responsibility. God, in His vast love and wisdom, created a space of self-reflection so that they could confront the truth within themselves.

In Genesis, Adam admits he is afraid because he is naked and then proceeds to blame the woman for making him eat the fruit. Just like the man by the pool of Bethesda blamed the people who would not take him to the pool, Adam blamed the woman.

"Do you want to be made well," and "Where are you?" are two questions we should ask ourselves. You may ask why. Especially if you have started the work of forgiveness.

I want to emphasize again if your rejection was rooted deeply, and for many of us it was, you will run into roadblocks, and it will take some extra work to dig out those roots. Your soul will want to do its job and continue to protect you. Part of the protection will want to move you back into the familiar. As you progress in this process, you must be intentional and allow your spirit to lead.

As we move through to the end of this healing journey, we must answer the question, "Do you want to be made well?" with a resounding "YES" daily. The question of "Where are you?" will also take consistent retrospection of your soul.

Be self-aware of where you are emotionally and mentally each and every day. If someone or something sets you off, and you begin to revert back to your old way of thinking, ask yourself, "Why?" What part of your wounded soul is being affected? This means it is an area that still "needs to be made well." Remember that forgiveness was a choice based on wanting to be set free, not a feeling.

The inclination will be to fall back into old patterns and pick up the resentment, anger, and bitterness. You may want to return to isolation and become distant from those you love. That's fine for a moment. But like the invalid, you have to get over your pity party, the exhausted excuses and take responsibility for your well-being. Once you recognize where you are, "GET UP AND WALK!"

It did not take a day, a month, or a year to get into the pit you found yourself in before you chose to break free. Restoration is a process; while it will take time, He will break the chains and help you overcome your past pain. In the end, you will be stronger for it, but you have to trust Him with the process. You and I are the reason Jesus gave His life; He wants to see you completely set free. The man by the pool of Bethesda was healed, but he still had to do his part.

LIVING IN FREEDOM

If you do find yourself taking backward steps, do not be too hard on yourself. You are human, and missteps are inevitable. However, just as you are working to fully forgive your offenders, forgive yourself if you do happen to falter. You are in the infancy stages of uncovering your true identity. Be patient with yourself. Be mindful that the need to rush the process also comes from past rejection. In fact, it was in the rejection that we learned to not accept ourselves.

The secret is consistency. Each day, you will have to remind yourself of how much God truly loves you. Accept who you are in the moment, and thank Him for restoring you to who He created you to be, even if it is not happening at the pace you would prefer. Fear will want to tell you the opposite: things will never change, or this is useless. Why bother?

Recognize the lie in your mind and combat it with the truth in His Word. Romans 12:2 reads, "Do not conform to the pattern of this world, but be transformed by the renewing of your mind." You have spent a long time allowing your mind to dictate your feelings and actions. This was because you were conforming to the beliefs and ideas created by your soul to protect you without even realizing it. Know this: some of the thinking your soul conjured up may have been accurate, but a lot of it probably was not. You must remember that believing those thoughts of the past has only served to steal a great deal of peace from your life.

Part of picking up your mat and walking is using your freedom, self-awareness, and intentionality to transform your mind instead. It is, without a doubt, the thoughts that determine our next move, so you want to be sure to stay on top of your thinking daily. This is different from thinking positively. While we all want to be positive and would like to avoid negativity as much as possible, positivity is a world-created conformity. The transformation of the mind mentioned in Romans 12:2 does not come from man but only through Jesus, cooperation with His Holy Spirit, and His Word.

SHINE LIGHT IN THE DARKNESS WITH HIS WORD

One of my favorite New Testament Bible books is John. For a mixture of reasons, it always causes a spiritual unraveling, no matter how many times my eyes read the first chapter.

> *"In the beginning was the Word, and the Word was with God, and the Word was God. He was in the beginning with God. All things came into being through Him, and apart from Him not even one thing came into being that has come into being. In Him was life, and the life was the Light of mankind. And the Light shines in the darkness, and the darkness did not grasp it"* (John 1:1–5 NASB).

If you are familiar with the Bible, you may notice John mirrors the beginning of this Gospel with the very first sentence of the book of Genesis, which reads, "In the beginning, God created the heavens and the earth." This holds great significance in the grand scheme of life, as you will see shortly.

Additionally, in his writings, it is clear that John understood that Jesus was distinct, yet still God, the Creator of all life, and that He had no beginning or end. There is also the magnitude of John referring to Jesus as the Word of God. It should be noted that this is not the only time. He does it again in 1 John 5:7 and Revelation 19:13. A bit later, in John 1:14, he adds, "And the Word became flesh and dwelt among us." There is no question that John is referring to Jesus. He wants the reader to be clear and in awe of the magnificence of Jesus, the Word of God.

He adds, "All things were made through Jesus, and without Him, nothing was made." Now, let us go back and tie that in with the very first book of the Old Testament. In the first chapter of Genesis, we read that God *spoke* the world into existence.

*"In the beginning, God **created** the heavens and the earth. And the earth was formless and desolate emptiness, and darkness was over the surface of the deep, and the Spirit of God was hovering over the surface of the waters. Then God **said**, 'Let there be light,' and there was light"* (Genesis 1:1–3 NASB, emphasis added).

Jesus was God's Voice, and the Voice held the ultimate power. This means the Word of God, Jesus, created light where there was once chaos and darkness.

Did you make the connection yet? The fabrications of your past come from a dark place. The lack of peace and joy you used to live in is proof of this. That dark place was never intended for you. When you allow the Word to shine light and prevail in the darkness, you will discover that peace and love will begin to govern and overwhelm those once-dark places.

Remember that the desire for connection was placed inside of us to be fulfilled by a relationship with our Creator, first. God speaks, connects, and communicates with His children in many ways, but the

Bible, His written Word, is the best way to get to know Him. And as you go through the process of being set free, it is the best way to get to know and love yourself. In the book of Hebrews, you find this truth:

"For the word of God is alive and active. Sharper than any double-edged sword, it penetrates even to dividing soul and spirit, joints and marrow; it judges the thoughts and attitudes of the heart" (4:12).

The realization of the power the Word holds is remarkable. You want to make reading the Word of God a daily habit. It is living and powerful because it is God's truth. It can break through to the deepest parts of your heart and bring to the surface the true you, laying bare your real intentions and honest thoughts.

The description of a double-edged sword and its ability to divide the soul and spirit is vital here. Throughout your life, the two have been woven together, pain and all. While your spirit has been regenerated, your soul has not. If you are open to it, what you encounter as you read will become spiritual healing for your soul and sustenance for your spirit. It is no different than feeding your body the right food to keep it healthy and strong. The Scriptures you come across will strengthen your spirit and turn your eyes toward the truth and goodness of God. The Apostle Paul puts it best:

"Summing it all up, friends, I'd say you'll do best by filling your minds and meditating on things true, noble, reputable, authentic, compelling, gracious—the best, not the worst; the beautiful, not the ugly; things to praise, not things to curse. Put into practice what you learned from me, what you heard and saw and realized. Do that and God, who makes everything work together, will work you into his most excellent harmonies" (Philippians 4:8–9, MSG).

The Word will keep you in check and honest with yourself when you ask the two questions, "Where are you, and do you want to be made well?" You want to do this consistently, but especially when you begin to feel the signs of defeat creeping in again, which is bound to happen.

REJECTION IS UNAVOIDABLE. HOW WILL YOU APPROACH IT?

The most essential truth about rejection that you absolutely need to get ahold of is that it is unavoidable. Unless you want to return to square one, you will have to accept that reality or risk finding yourself back in the mental misery you lived in before you elected to be set free.

You want to be ready for any future rejection in your healing journey. Part of true freedom for some will come with the desire to put yourself out there, which can make you more susceptible to being rejected. Remember that just because you are free does not mean others are, too.

Most broken people are not even aware of the position they are in. Likely, some are not even interested in knowing. That is not your problem. You need to get out of the habit of relying on others to meet your needs. While you will find that as you walk through this healing journey of freedom, your relationships with the people you love will begin to flourish and become healthier, you cannot put expectations on them to make you feel better. They are human, and they will let you down. Let God fill those places in your heart as only He can.

When, and not if, you run into rejection again, you must refuse to receive the feelings and thoughts that want to slither back inside your mind. Be aware that it is your soul responding by trying to tie you back up to the post again. The last thing you need is to start piling up the garbage you used to carry around. Remember, you are the one who loses joy and peace.

When rejection does show up at your door again, kindly smile, dust off your shoes, and walk away. Thank God for what He has brought you out of. If the Holy Spirit brings the offender to mind during time spent with Him, say a prayer for the person. As horrible as they may be, God wants them set free, too.

LOVE IS THE KEY

In the book of Mark, Jesus is asked which is the greatest commandment. He responds by giving the first and generously adds the second as well. The first is, *"Love the Lord your God with all your heart and with all your soul and with all your mind and with all your strength"* (12:30).

If you spend time in His Word, this commandment will come easy for you. Reading consistently, even in small doses, will strengthen the restorative process and bring you the peace you deserve. You will find healing for your soul through the life-giving promises you encounter. His Word will point you in the right direction each and every day, and you will come to know your Heavenly Father in a way you never thought possible.

The second commandment is a bit more challenging as Jesus adds, "Love your neighbor as yourself." The beauty here is that the more we love God and accept His love for us, the more we are set free and are led to love the people around us. While it sounds easy enough, the problem for many who have experienced deep-seated rejection is that while they can attest to their love for God and others, they often cannot fully receive the love God has for them.

Whether you realize it or not, this inability to receive His love completely, comes from our past rejection. If we do not address it, it will very likely cause a breakdown in the connection with others. It will not be blatantly evident since you will undoubtedly be at a higher and healthier level in your relationships than before. But trust me when I tell you, you will miss out on receiving the full abundance referred to throughout these chapters and in His Word. The dilemma is that intellectually, it is understood that God loves us, but accepting that love fully is a different story. It is similar to receiving forgiveness.

Our human mind, the thinking part of us, will often want to compare how God loves us to the way people have loved us. Yet, there is no comparison. The people who attempted to love or said they loved us negatively impacted our souls through their words, actions, and disregard. They rejected us, and that began carving the negative ravine of feeling unwanted and unworthy in our souls. In response, we reacted in a way that would protect us, either by trying to do "better" so we would be accepted or by "freezing them out" emotionally and mentally to avoid further pain. Those subconscious actions kept us running on a treadmill of survival, and we got nowhere.

SOUL ALIGNMENT

We must remember we are humans, and the people who hurt us are too. They were also adversely affected by their own broken people and, at some point, felt similarly to the way they made us feel. They have been on that same treadmill without knowing it.

Sadly, this is how much of humanity functions. The pattern disrupts relationships everywhere, at the very least, and is frequently repeated through generations. Yet, there is no denying that if you ask the rejectors and those who have suffered at their hands if they felt love, you will get a definite "Yes" from many on either side. While it is far from what love is meant to be, it is the only love we have known. This is why, for many of us, there is a disconnection and a misunderstanding when it comes to accepting God's love for us.

God's love is nothing like the love we have experienced; it is often beyond our human comprehension. I have often tried to make sense of it by looking at the love a parent has for a child, but I believe even this misses the mark. If you recall the words penned by John in his first chapter, he knew Jesus personally. He essentially referred to himself as "the disciple whom Jesus loved" (John 21:20). Be reminded there were other disciples, but he was the only one who described himself in this way, and he did it more than once.

This does not mean Jesus did not love the other disciples. It was simply evidence that John clearly understood the unconditional love he directly experienced from Jesus, and he accepted that love with great joy. He understood Jesus' transformative love so well that he was loyal to the end. Jesus' love changed his entire life. It was because of this love, the same love He has for you and me, that John found his purpose and true identity.

The Apostle Paul, like John, also understood God's love, and he prayed that the people of Ephesus would be able to grasp the riches of it all. He wrote about that love in Ephesians 3:14–21:

"For this reason I kneel before the Father, from whom every family in heaven and on earth derives its name. I pray that out of his glorious riches he may strengthen you with power through his Spirit in your inner being, so that Christ may dwell in your hearts through faith. And I pray that you, being rooted and established in love, may have power, together with all the Lord's holy people, to grasp how wide and long and high and deep is the love of Christ, and to know this love that surpasses knowledge—that you may be filled to the measure of all the fullness of God. Now to him who is able to do immeasurably more than all we ask or imagine, according to his power that is at work within us, to him be glory in the church and in Christ Jesus throughout all generations, forever and ever! Amen"

In order to move forward and live the life of abundance promised by Jesus, it is crucial to know where the disconnection occurs. You may ask, "Why is this beautiful gift of unconditional love hard for some of us to grasp?" You have to remember that we were created as a three-part being. We are a spirit that lives in a body, and we have a soul. In the words of Watchman Nee, "God dwells in the spirit, self dwells in the soul, while senses dwell in the body." The spirit gives life to our body. It is the logical part of us, and it alone can grasp the things of God. It is our spirit that holds the highest potential of our very being.

When we surrender our life to Jesus, our spirit is reborn. His Spirit awakens and ignites our spirit, and many seem to walk around on cloud nine because there is a sudden awareness of what was once incomprehensible. This is why people will describe a sense of euphoria when they accept Jesus into their lives. Many attest to experiencing an overwhelming love at this first encounter. It is as if your spirit recognizes that the Father is finally home. There appears to be an automatic alignment of our spirit to His. However, the same cannot be said about our souls. Our mind, our will, and our emotions often do not fall into position in the same way.

You see, for most of our lives, our body has been directed by the soul and the desires of our flesh. They need to be transformed, too. This is why dividing the spirit and soul with the double-edged sword of the Word of God is vital to total restoration.

The problem lies with the patterns of our old wrong thinking. This is the same wrong thinking that comes out of the ravine of misery carved into our minds. The same wrong thinking got us to the place where we were void of joy and peace, and for many of us, it has been cutting a deeper gap consistently throughout our entire lives. This warped thinking comes from the soul. While in the beginning, we are in a state of bliss because our spirit is leading us, if we do not learn how to "take up our mat and walk" by willingly allowing the spirit to continue to lead, we can and will fall back into our old corrupt comfort zone.

YOU ARE WORTHY

In our human nature, at the first sign of uncertainty, the mind, will, and emotions grab back the reigns, and the soul begins to lead once again. There is then an ongoing battle in the seat of our hearts. We beat ourselves up because we believe we have failed, self-condemnation sets in, and the voice of our soul tells us we are not worthy of His love. So, it is understandable how the second greatest commandment will give us trouble.

The thoughts, beliefs, and ideas created in our souls are infused with painful memories, and when our injured heart is in charge, it reverts to that pain of the past. This causes the deep canyons formerly dug into our souls by the shame and unworthiness of our past rejections to set off alarms when even the faintest sign of potential heartache appears.

Again, the soul wants to protect you, so its message is that it is too risky and inadvertently and ironically rejects all love, including the love of God. Therefore, because we have not allowed our soul to be dealt with, fear and shame creep in again. We silence the joy of the spirit and cannot fathom that the God of all creation can love us in such a marvelous way.

While we can love those God has blessed our lives with better than before, we hit a ceiling because our minds cannot accept the Ultimate Love. In turn, this means we cannot fully love ourselves. We say we do and act in such a way as to prove it to the world and ourselves. However, I must note that loving yourself here is not what you read about in magazines or hear on countless podcasts.

Social media and Hollywood have singlehandedly persuaded the masses to surrender to the cult of self-love. At every turn, the self-help gurus shout that the key to happiness is to love ourselves. Do not get me wrong; I am all about loving thyself. Especially when it is a biblical command. While self-love is an integral part of living an abundant life, the reality is that the self-love you see all over the internet in the form of selfies is often a façade.

Truly loving yourself happens through the courageous uncovering and recognition of who God has created you to be. Accepting the fact that despite the pain and hurt caused by rejection, you are worthy of love and respect. You consider yourself enough to take care of your whole self: your body, your spirit, and your soul.

I will repeat this once again: God's love is not like the world's love. It will never compare. You have to grasp that there is no point system. He does not love you because you are good. You have it all wrong. It is because He loves you that He makes you good.

If you are going to do this, do it wholeheartedly. Give Him your entire being (body, soul, and spirit), and He will do the rest. Picking up your mat and walking means utilizing your will (the will that is part of your soul) to make the ultimate decision to allow the Word of God to conquer and heal your soul and put your faith into action by freely accepting and receiving His amazing love for you.

1 John 4:8 clearly tells us, "God is love!" Love is who He is. That is a straight-up fact, whether you feel His love or not. The fear you continue to allow to live in your soul drives you away from receiving His love. Only His perfect love will cast out that fear (1 John 4:18). He sees you and I through that love and loves us more than we could ever imagine. You must trust Him and believe the way John believed; He loves you, too.

ALWAYS REMEMBER, YOU GET TO CHOOSE

The goal is to get to the place where you are no longer giving power to the things of your past. Dr. Henry Cloud refers to this as "necessary endings." He emphasizes the fact that to get to tomorrow, you have to put an end to today.

The reality is that all things, good and bad, will, without question, come to an end at some point in our lives.

Reread that sentence and ponder the thought for a moment. Yesterday is over, and tomorrow is not yet here. Yet, the regrets of the past and the anxiety for the future keep those negative emotions alive. And guess what? We are doing that to ourselves because we continue to replay incidents that are already done with and scenarios that have yet to take place over and over in our mind, like a broken record. So we live missing out on the best of today.

The takeaway I adopted from this knowledge is that "the good things should be appreciated and enjoyed, for I will not have them forever."

On that same note, the bad things need to be sifted out as soon as possible so they do not have the power to take away my time and energy from all the good things and people that bless my life. With this in mind, why not end the things that bring me misery as soon as possible on my own terms?

Your emotional attachment to the hurts of your past will only keep you from moving into the total restoration of your future.

You may find that you move three steps forward and two steps back, and on rough days, you might only take two steps forward and fall back four or five. That's okay; give yourself grace. You have been through a lot, and most of your life has been lived through a defeated way of thinking.

However, never attempt to sugarcoat it. Remember to ask yourself, "Do you want to be made well, and where are you?" But you have to be honest about your progress.

Think of the rejection wounds you carried as excess body weight you are trying to lose. It would be best to consider how much weight you want to get rid of to get to a healthy state. In this comparison, the more hurt you carry, the more pounds you need to shed. Someone who only has twenty pounds to lose will not have the same battle as someone who needs to lose two hundred to get their health on track. Every weight loss journey has struggles and setbacks. But six months down the road, if you have only managed to lose ten percent of the weight intended, it should be evident that something is not working. You need to reevaluate your consumption and activity.

This is similar to your emotional healing journey. The deeper the emotional ravine in your soul is, the more intentionality and effort you will need to put into your healing journey.

Rely on His Word, surround yourself with people who build you up, and detach yourself from those who bring you down. Do not take anything personally. Be reminded that neither those who love and accept you nor those who disapprove and reject you define who you are. Only God does that, and accepting His love for you is the most powerful Counselor your wounded heart will ever meet. Give Him His place in your life, be patient with yourself, and give yourself the love and grace you have always deserved.

Each day is a new day; examine it closely and appreciate the gifts it brings. Enjoy getting to know the real you daily. Embrace the blessings, whether they are big or small. Even in the midst of challenges that will come up, treasures are waiting to be discovered by you. While rejection is part of our world, it does not have the power to define you anymore unless you allow it. Cast aside the shackles of rejection, grab hold of His promises, and rise up. Pick up your mat and walk!

THE BUMMER LAMB

*Every once in a while, a ewe will give birth to a lamb and reject
it. There are many reasons she may do this. If the lamb is returned
to the ewe, the mother may even kick the poor animal away. Once
a ewe rejects one of her lambs, she will never change her mind.*

*These little lambs will hang their head so low that it looks like something
is wrong with its neck. Their spirit is broken. These lambs are called
"bummer lambs." Unless the shepherd intervenes, that lamb will
die, rejected and alone. So, do you know what the shepherd does?*

*He takes that rejected little one into his home, hand-feeds it and keeps it
warm by the fire. He will wrap it up with blankets and hold it to his chest
so the bummer can hear his heartbeat. Once the lamb is strong enough,
the shepherd will place it back in the field with the rest of the flock.*

*But that sheep never forgets how the shepherd cared for
him when his mother rejected him. When the shepherd
calls for the flock, guess who runs to him first?*

That is right, the bummer sheep. He knows his voice intimately.

*It is not that the bummer lamb is loved more, it
just knows intimately the one who loves it.*

*It's not that it is loved more, it just believes it because
it has experienced that love, one on one.*

*So many of us are bummer lambs, rejected and broken. But
He is the good Shepherd. He cares for our every need and
holds us close to His heart so we can hear His heartbeat.*

We may be broken but we are deeply loved by the Shepherd.

AUTHOR UNKNOWN

For I know the plans I have for you, declares the Lord, plans to prosper you, and not harm you, plans to give you hope and a future. Then you will call on me and come and pray to me, and I will listen to you. You will seek me and find me when you seek me with all your heart.

JEREMIAH 29:11-13

APPENDIX

ADVERSE CHILDHOOD EXPERIENCE (ACE) QUESTIONNAIRE

This questionnaire asks 10 questions about events that may have happened during your childhood, up until the first 18 years of your life. Your responses will allow you to better understand how problems that occurred during your early life may impact the challenges you face today.

While you were growing up:

1. Did a parent or other adult in your household often:

   Swear at you, insult you, put you down, or humiliate you?
   or
   Act in a way that made you afraid that you might be physically hurt?

   Enter 1, if yes _____

2. Did a parent or other adult in the household often:

   Push, grab, slap, or throw something at you?
   or
   Ever hit you so hard that you had marks or were injured?

   Enter 1, if yes _____

3. Did an adult or person at least 5 years older than you ever:

   Touch or fondle you or have you touch their body in a sexual way?
   or
   Attempt or actually have intercourse with you?

   Enter 1, if yes _____

4. Did you often feel that:

   No one in your family loved you or though you were important or special?
   or
   Your family did not look out for each other, feel close to each other or support each other?

   Enter 1, if yes _____

5. Did you often feel that:

   You did not have enough to eat, had to wear dirty clothes, and had no one to protect you?
   or
   Your parents were too drunk or high to take care of you or take you to the doctor when needed?

   Enter 1, if yes _____

6. Were your parents ever separated or divorced?

   Enter 1, if yes _____

7. Were any of your parents or adult caregivers:

   Often pushed, grabbed, slapped, or had something thrown at them?
   or
   Sometimes or often kicked, bitten, hit with a fist, or other objects?
   or
   Every repeatedly hit over at least a few minutes or threatened with a gun or knife?

   Enter 1, if yes _____

8. Did you live with anyone who was a problem drinker or alcoholic, or who used street drugs?

   Enter 1, if yes _____

9. Was a household member depressed or mentally ill, or did a household member attempt suicide?

   Enter 1, if yes _____

10. Did a household member go to prison?

   Enter 1, if yes _____

Total Yes Responses: _____

0–3 *low risk for health concerns associated with adverse childhood experiences*

4–5 *moderate risk for health concerns associated with adverse childhood experiences*

6–10 *high risk for health concerns associated with adverse childhood experiences*

This is not a complete list of factors that contribute to childhood toxic stress, since it does not take into consideration issues that occur outside the home. Also, the assessment does not take into consideration positive factors, such as having another trusted family or community member create a safe environment, thus buffering the toxic effects. Therefore, the ACE score is not a diagnostic tool.

The cardiovascular system, immune system, and the developing brain are all known to be at particular risk from ongoing toxic stress. Studies show a correlation between people who sustained high toxic stress levels in their early years and having certain physical and mental illnesses later in life. It is important to note that there are people who score high on the test and live healthy lives.

REFERENCES

Amen, Daniel, G. *The End of Mental Illness: How Neuroscience Is Transforming Psychiatry and Helping Prevent or Reverse Mood and Anxiety Disorders, ADHD, Addictions, PTSD, Psychosis, Personality Disorders, and More*. Carol Stream, Illinois: Tyndale Momentum, 2020.

American Heart Association. "Is Broken Heart Syndrome Real?" 2021. https://www.heart.org/en/health-topics/cardiomyopathy/what-is-cardiomyopathy-in-adults/is-broken-heart-syndrome-real.

Ardiel, Evan L, and Catharine H Rankin. "The Importance of Touch in Development." *Paediatrics & Child Health* 15, no. 3 (2010): 153–156. doi:10.1093/pch/15.3.153.

Berkman, Lisa F. and S. Leonard Syme. "Social Networks, Host Resistance, and Mortality: A Nine-Year Follow-up Study of Alameda County Residents." *American Journal of Epidemiology* 109 (1979): 186–204.

Brogaard, Berit, PhD. "Parental Attachment Problems: Child Neglect and Its Consequences." *Psychology Today* November 9, 2016. https://www.psychologytoday.com/us/blog/the-mysteries-love/201611/parental-attachment-problems-child-neglect-and-its-consequences.

Clinton, Tim and Ron Hawkins. *The Quick Reference Guide to Biblical Counseling*. Grand Rapids: Baker Books, 2009.

Cloud, Henry. *Necessary Endings: The Employees, Businesses, and Relationships That All of Us Have to Give Up in Order to Move Forward.* Nashville: HarperCollins Leadership, 2010.

Clowes, Brian. "The Miracle of Fetal Development: A Pro-Life Weapon." Human Life International, 2021, https://www.hli.org/resources/miracle-fetal-development/.

Cook, Gareth. "Why We Are Wired to Connect". *Scientific American* October 22, 2013. https://www.scientificamerican.com/article/why-we-are-wired-to-connect/.

Dewar, Gwen, Ph.D. "Spanking Babies: Is It Okay to Spank an Infant?" *Parenting Science*, 2019. https://www.parentingscience.com/spanking-babies.html.

Gershoff, E. T. et al. "Spanking and Child Development: We Know Enough Now to Stop Hitting Our Children." *Child Development Perspectives* 7(3) (2013): 133–137.

Goleman, Daniel. "The Experience of Touch: Research Points to a Critical Role." *New York Times*, February 2, 1988. https://www.nytimes.com/1988/02/02/science/the-experience-of-touch-research-points-to-a-critical-role.html.

Goleman, Daniel. "Researchers Trace Empathy's Roots to Infancy." *New York Times*, August 8, 1989.

Goleman, Daniel. *Emotional Intelligence: Why It Can Matter More than IQ.* New York: Bantam Bell, 2005.

Gorski, T. Terrence. *Getting Love Right: Learning the Choices of Healthy Intimacy.* New York: Fireside, 1993.

Gracia, E. Lila M. and G. Musitu. "Parental Rejection and Psychosocial Adjustment of Children." *Salud Mental,* 2(41) (2005): 73–81.

Holmes, Thomas H. and Richard H. Rahe. "The Social Readjustment Rating Scale." *Journal of Psychosomatic Research* 11 (1967): 213–218.

Hunt, June. *How to Rise above Abuse: Victory for Victims of Five Types of Abuse.* Eugene, Oregon: Harvest House Publishers, 2010.

Jackson, John Paul. *Breaking Free of Rejection.* North Sutton, New Hampshire: Streams Publishing House, 2004.

Johnson, Sue and Kenneth Sanderfer. *Created for Connection: The Hold Me Tight Guide for Christian Couples.* New York: Hatchet Book Groups, 2016.

Meyer, Joyce. *Beauty for Ashes: Receiving Emotional Healing.* New York: Hatchette Book Group, 2003.

Muday, Gloria K., and Heather Brown-Harding. "Abstract of Nervous System-like Signaling in Plant Defense." *Science* 361, no. 6407 (September 2018): 1068–1069.

Nakazawa, Donna, J. *Childhood Disrupted: How Your Biography Becomes Your Biology, and How You Can Heal.* New York: Simon & Schuster, Inc., 2015.

Nee, Watchman. *The Spiritual Man.* New York: Christian Fellowship Publishers, 1977.

Nelson, Charles A., et al. "Adversity in Childhood Is Linked to Mental and Physical Health throughout Life." *BMJ (Clinical research ed.)* 371, 2020: m3048. doi:10.1136/bmj.m3048. PMID: 33115717; PMCID: PMC7592151.

Rohner, Ronald P. "Parental Acceptance-Rejection Theory and the Phylogenetic Model." Files.Eric.Ed.Gov, 2021. Accessed July 16, 2021, https://files.eric.ed.gov/fulltext/ED151718.pdf.

Ryan, Richard M., and Robert Kuczkowski. "The Imaginary Audience, Self-Consciousness, and Public Individuation in Adolescence." *Journal of Personality* 62, no. 2 (1994): 219–238. doi: 10.1111/j.1467-6494.1994.tb00292.x.

SACAP. "Applied Psychology: The Difference between Empathy and Sympathy (And How to Nurture Both)." 2018. Accessed September 2020, https://www.sacap.edu.za/blog/applied-psychology/empathy-vs-sympathy/.

Skeen, Michelle, PsyD. "Love Me, Don't Leave Me." The Refuge, March 21, 2019. https://www.therefuge-ahealingplace.com/ptsd-treatment/abandonment/.

Tannenbaum, Melanie. "The Incredible Importance of Mom." *Scientific American*, Blog Network. 2021. Accessed July 8, 2021, https://blogs.scientificamerican.com/psysociety/mothers-day-2013/.

University of Rochester Medical Center. "Blood Circulation in the Fetus and Newborn." University Of Rochester Medical Center Health Encyclopedia, 2021. https://www.urmc.rochester.edu/encyclopedia/content.aspx?ContentTypeID=90&ContentID=P02362.

Verny, Thomas and John Kelly. *The Secret Life of the Unborn Child: How You Can Prepare Your Unborn Baby for a Happy, Healthy Life.* New York: Bantam Dell Publishing Group, 1981.

Winch, Guy, Ph.D. *Emotional First Aid: Healing Rejection, Guilt, Failure and Other Everyday Hurts.* New York: Hudson Street Press, 2013.

Wright, H. Norman. *Crisis and Trauma Counseling.* Minneapolis: Bethany House, 2009.

ABOUT THE AUTHOR

Melissa Cade Garcia, a dedicated lifelong educator, shines as a prominent figure in the fields of coaching, consulting, and counseling. Her exceptional career, spanning over two decades, has allowed her to channel her extensive experience into igniting progress in leadership development, promoting behavioral awareness, and enriching academic circles. Melissa's remarkable journey has unfolded against the scenic backdrop of Southwest Florida, where she resides with her husband, David, and two wonderful children, Jonas and Kayla.

As a Certified Coach with the esteemed John Maxwell Team and a respected DISC Consultant, Melissa has guided countless individuals and groups on their own transformative journeys. Her mission is simple yet deeply impactful: to shatter barriers and build bridges that lead others toward their personal and professional goals. Her expertise as a Behavior Analyst, Brain Health Coach, and lifelong Educator, combined with a master's degree in Pastoral Counseling, has equipped her to approach clients and students with a holistic perspective on the human soul.

In her role as the visionary behind Transformative Connections, clients gain the necessary tools (and insights) to navigate change, cultivate innovation, and foster a culture of excellence in their respective spheres of influence. Her passion for education and empowerment extends globally through her platform, where she ignites positive change, inspires innovation, and nurtures cultures of excellence in people's lives worldwide.

Melissa Cade Garcia's tireless dedication, profound knowledge, and remarkable gift for cultivating growth in others leave an enduring mark on her clients and students. If you are ready to embark on an exceptional journey of self-discovery, personal development, or professional success, reach out and connect to set the course for your own transformation.

Discover explosive growth and reach new heights through the POWER of connection!

Your journey toward authentic leadership begins here. Connect with us, and together, let's unlock your true potential, revolutionize your sphere of influence, and leave a lasting legacy of transformation!

Use the QR code below to schedule a complimentary fifteen-minute discovery call.

Whether you're an educator trying to gain control in the classroom, a professional ready to take your career and team to a new level, or an individual eager to unlock the POWER of CONNECTION for personal growth, explore how we can tailor our services to meet your needs. Visit our website today for more information:

Transformativeconnections.net

Check out some of these transformational products on our website under the "Services & Resources" tab or scan the QR code below:

The POWER of Self-Connection

A Transformative Self-Help Guide, Interactive Workbook, & Journal with a Gratitude Log

Get your copy of our brand new 4-in-1 downloadable eBook

Coming Soon!!

The highly anticipated

The Reality of Rejection Bible Study Guide

Join our notification list on our page and receive a complimentary

Self-Connection Journal & Gratitude Log

eBook copy

Printed in the USA
CPSIA information can be obtained
at www.ICGtesting.com
LVHW011529050124
767941LV00091B/4922